The

Million

Dollar

Coach

by Dowaun Proctor & Adolfo Morales

COPYRIGHT AND DISCLAIMER

Dowaun Proctor & Adolfo Morales

Published by:
Leader Publishing Worldwide
19 Axford Bay
Port Moody, BC V3H 3R4
Tel: 1 888 294 9151
Fax: 1 877 575 9151
Website: www.noresults-nofee.com

DEDICATION

I would like to dedicate this book to my staff. I admire your hard work and the creativity you put towards our small business and our clients. I have taken many things you've implemented and put them into this book. A huge thank you to my COO & Business Partner, Adolfo Morales, for your understanding of the time it takes to write a book, and believing that we can do this. I hope this makes you proud.

CONTENTS

INTRODUCTION

This is the first page, but by opening this book you have already taken an important step towards increasing the success of your business. Congratulations on your quest to enhance your business and marketing skills.

When I put pen to paper, or keyboard to Word document, I found myself with an enormous amount of useful marketing material which I've used since 1998. This experience is drawn from many different business entities including: ownership and management in 3 restaurants, owner of a delivery company, small business consulting company, financial services and insurance company, and E-Commerce website(s). Several of these I continue to own, but consult from afar. The strategies I talk about in this book are still in place at these companies.

Even though I truly believe we are all 1 or 2 great marketing ideas away from more sales opportunities than we can fully imagine, I believe the first two chapters are as important as the following eight. The strategies in this book - when implemented with strategy and care - are guaranteed to make you more money with less effort. These are strategies that have helped businesses just like yours make hundreds of thousands of dollars more - including your competitors. These strategies have created several multi-million dollar businesses.

This is the reason I have dedicated my life to Business Consulting. Since starting my company to provide direction for small business operators, I have been literally overwhelmed with the demand for marketing, structure, and accountability. Most importantly has been the need of small business operators to surround themselves with someone that cares and can provide a proper and profitable third party perspective.

As you follow the book and read the principles to follow, remember it does not matter what industry, nor type of business you operate (I've been a part of many). What matters is that you grasp the heart of the principles, the underlying lessons and strategies, that can help grow any operation in any category of business imaginable.

Yours in Success,

~ Dowaun Proctor & Adolfo Morales

PS. If you would like to arrange a meeting to get a profitable third party perspective on your business, please send an email to: morales.adolfo.h@gmail.com and we will gladly point you in the right direction.

1

Create Added Value in Your Business

and Make $1 + 1 = 3$

The majority of small businesses, like yours, are established in response to market demand for a product or service. Many build their businesses by serving that demand, and enjoy growing profits without putting much effort into long-term planning or marketing.

However, what happens when that demand slows or stops? What happens when the competition sets up shop with a "new and improved" version of your product down the road? How do you keep your offering fresh, while growing and maintaining your client base? The answer is by adding value to your product or service.

Added value is a marketing or customer relations strategy that can take the form of a product, service, which is added to the original offering for free, or as part of a discounted package. It, like all other elements in your marketing

To learn the 3 biggest mistakes all business owners make and how to avoid them, visit www.ballistamanagement.com

toolkit, is designed to attract new customers and retain existing ones. A simple example of added value would be if you owned a gift shop, and offered complimentary gift wrapping with every purchase.

If you don't refresh and renew your offering over time, your customers will get bored and be drawn to your competitor. Your employees, too, may become disinterested, and find work elsewhere. Ultimately, both clients and employees will demand additional value to remain loyal – and aren't they the keystones for your business growth?

Can You Add Value to Your Business?

Everyone can add value to their business. Better yet, everyone can *afford* to add value to their business. Adding value doesn't have to blow your marketing budget, or take up hours of your time. There are many ways – big and small – to enhance your business in the eyes of your clients.

The key to adding value is determining what your customers and target market perceive as valuable. You must understand their needs, wants, troubles and inconveniences in order to entice them with solutions through added value products or services. Adding value will add to your profits, but if you don't focus on genuinely helping your clients, you'll have a difficult time attracting them.

Added value works for both product- and service-based businesses. If you offer a service, like hairstyling, try treating your customers with products like a latte while they wait, shampoo samples, or a free conditioning treatment with every sixth visit. If you sell a product, consider offering convenience

2

services – like free shipping or delivery – to make the customer's experience a seamless one. The customer will feel appreciated and their needs will have been taken care of.

Ways to Add Value to Your Business

There are many ways to enhance your offer, depending on your budget and the resources you have access to. You may wish to hold a brainstorming session with your staff to come up with ideas for your business; if your employees are on the front lines, they'll likely have firsthand information about what clients would like to see more of.

Feature Your Expertise

Your intellectual property is a free resource that you have at your disposal to share with your clients. This will make them feel as though they have an inside track. You might want to consider adding it to your business, making it a value-added service.

Expert corner: Supplement your website and newsletter with columns on topics of interest to your customers and of relevance to your service. This will position you as an expert in the marketplace, and give your clients helpful information they won't receive from the competition.

Do It Yourself Tips: This is a great tool for seasonal marketing. Provide your clients with this information on your website, in your newsletters, or on take away note cards in your store or office. Ideas include recipes, craft ideas, gift ideas – all of which are branded with your company logo and contact information, and include your product as an ingredient.

To learn the 3 biggest mistakes all business owners make and how to avoid them, visit www.ballistamanagement.com

What to Expect Tips: Take your customer through what they should expect in the first few days (weeks) of using your service or product, and how they can make the most of it. This can include assembly instructions, product care and cleaning, or service results (like a 25% increase in business – guaranteed!).

Related + Community Events: Own a store that sells athletic equipment? Post information on your website, in store, and in your newsletter about upcoming races, games, or consumer trade shows. Or simply keep a bulletin in your office of community events and offers that will draw your clients in, and establish itself as a hub in the neighborhood for information.

Offer Convenience Services

Customer service is a dying practice in our high paced culture – use it to your advantage. When done well, it can be the difference between you and the competition, or the deciding factor for a potential repeat client.

Envision the steps involved for a customer to arrive at your store, purchase your offering, and use your product or service. Can you eliminate any of those steps for them? Can you shorten waiting times, or make them more pleasurable? Stepping into your clients' shoes will allow you to determine the most powerful value add for your company. Here are a few ideas:

Free Delivery + Shipping: With clearly established parameters (will you ship your product free to India?), this is a solid value added service that many businesses offer. Free delivery (usually with a purchase over a set

4

amount) is a huge convenience for many people who do not have access to a vehicle, or need help moving large items.

Follow up Services: This works great for computers, appliances and other mechanical or technology-based products. Offer maintenance and service contracts for three time periods; instead of dealing with the manufacturer, customers will rely on you for assistance which brings them back into the store and establishes a relationship of trust.

Gift-Wrapping: A great service to provide – especially for seasonal gifts. This service costs very little, and can have a big impact on your customer's experience.

"While You Wait" Amenities: If you could make your customer feel like a VIP for minimal cost, why wouldn't you? Offering amenities like coffee and treats, free samples and services (wireless internet is a big one) will go a long way.

Comparison-Shopping Tools: Show your customers that you are so sure your product will measure up against the competition, that you'll help them compare.

Establish Complementary Partnerships

Complementary partnerships with other businesses can take you a long way toward adding value for your customer, and generating new business. Just like a joint testimonial mailing, the power (and convenience) of referral business is immense.

5

To learn the 3 biggest mistakes all business owners make and how to avoid them, visit www.ballistamanagement.com

Build a web of associates: If you're a yoga instructor, carry the cards of your treatment providers (physiotherapists, massage therapists, etc.) to refer your students to. In exchange, your brochure or card is posted in their offices. This works for automotive repair, esthetics, consultants and other service providers. Customers will trust referrals received by their existing service providers, and feel taken care of by a reputable community of experts.

Establish partnerships with financial incentives: This is one that has your interests in mind as well as your customers'. In addition to establishing a complementary partnership with a related associate, establish an incentive structure where each of you are compensated for your referrals. For example, if you refer a client to a furniture store after they've purchased a mattress from you, and they buy a bed frame, your associate will pay you a portion of the sale – and vice versa.

Location-based partnerships: Consider creating partnerships with the businesses around you – even if your products and services don't appear to be related. Shopping malls do this all the time with value coupon books that customers must purchase for $5 to $20 dollars. These partnerships and incentives will keep the customer spending money in the area, which is good for everyone's bottom line.

Packages + Bundles

Packaging and bundling products and services is one of the most popular methods of adding value. Clients perceive the bundles as having a higher value than the sum of the individual items – or as receiving something for free.

To learn the 3 biggest mistakes all business owners make and how to avoid them, visit www.ballistamanagement.com

Cleverly packaged and named bundles can spark interest and revive your products in the eyes of your customers. Remember to always give the offers an end date or provide a limited number to create a sense of scarcity and urgency and to prevent this strategy from going stale.

Intuitive product bundles: Package independent related products together, and give them a reduced price or name. For example, this could be selling an extra pair of running socks with new running shoes. Remember the convenience of starter kits – package everything your customer will need to begin a new activity – painting, camping, running, etc. – in a bundle for simple buying decisions.

Package your upsell: This can also be called a chain of purchasing. It includes the products or services your client will need to use your product or service. Won't they need leather protector for their new boots? If they've run out of oil paints, how's their supply of brushes, acrylics or canvases? By packaging these clearly related products together, you are making their shopping experience faster and more convenient.

Offer a Customer Loyalty Program

There are a number of ways to structure your rewards and loyalty program, depending on the type of business and level of technological resources available to you. Customer loyalty programs have a huge advantage – they help build your database of customer information and in most cases allow you to view and analyze purchasing patterns. Here are the most popular:

To learn the 3 biggest mistakes all business owners make and how to avoid them, visit www.ballistamanagement.com

Every 6th (or 10th) Visit on Us: This works well for business that rely on repeat visits from their customers – like hair salons, coffee shops, auto maintenance, etc. Customers receive a card with store information on the front, and space for stamps or initials on the back. Remember that while 10 is a nice even number, it may be too far in the future for some customers (especially for services that are three to six weeks apart). The idea of six visits is more manageable.

Rewards Dollars: This is the Canadian Tire model. For every dollar your customer spends in store, they receive a small portion back in store credit (i.e., Canadian Tire money). The store credit is in the form of printed dollars, branded with your company logo and contact information, and serves as a reminder each time a client opens their wallet.

Rewards Points: Another common value-add strategy is a rewards points system. Most grocery stores use this incentive, as well as credit card companies. This works the same as rewards dollars, where a certain number of points are accumulated based on each dollar spent in store. Points can then be spent in store, or on products you have brought in for "rewards points holders" only. This strategy also allows you to feature products with "extra points value" instead of discounting prices.

Membership Amenities: Instead of points or dollars, you can offer VIP treatment for members, when they sign up for or purchase a membership. This may include occasional discounts, but is primarily centered around perks like "while you wait" amenities, skipping the line, free delivery, etc. You can also produce membership cards.

8

To learn the 3 biggest mistakes all business owners make and how to avoid them, visit www.ballistamanagement.com

Final Thoughts

One of the mistakes many businesses make after reading this list is attempting to implement too many projects at one time. Each one of these ideas, individually, can help you generate revenue. Begin with one idea. Implement it. Gauge the response. Then decide if you should keep it or not. This process may take a while depending on your sales cycle. That's ok. Once you have decided if you are keeping of scrapping the idea, then begin implementing a second idea.

With your second idea, what we have found works best, is planning it during the implementation of the first. By having a plan in place before you decide to implement, mistakes can be avoided. Planning also provides time for you and your team to figure out how to maximize the effectiveness of the idea.

Client Testimonial

"When I first met Dowuan, I was not sure that they could help my business out. As a salon owner, I thought there were not many methods to attract clients. He took the time to listen to my situation and only recommended I make one change. After making that change, I was quickly surprised by how many new clients were coming in! It did not take a long time to see the results."

~C. P.

To learn the 3 biggest mistakes all business owners make and how to avoid them, visit www.ballistamanagement.com

2

Creating Effective

Marketing Material

Your marketing collateral gets sent out in the world to do one thing: act as an ambassador for your product or service, in place of *you*. This may seem like a big job for a piece of paper, but it's a helpful way to think about the materials you create.

When you meet with a potential or existing client, you do a number of things. You make sure you are well prepared with all the information the customer could need. You dress in clothing that is appropriate. You anticipate their needs, and offer a solution to their problems. You may also cater to how they best like to receive information.

Chances are, you wouldn't meet with clients just for the sake of meeting with a client – say, for instance, to show off your new suit. Likewise, you shouldn't create and distribute collateral that is non-essential.

To learn the 3 biggest mistakes all business owners make and how to avoid them, visit www.ballistamanagement.com

We all know that the biggest challenge for small businesses is the limited number of zeros attached to their marketing budget. Marketing materials can be expensive, and a single, well-produced piece has the ability to devour the entire budget. Given that billion-dollar marketing campaigns fail every day, how can you be sure to make the most of, and be successful with, the dollars you're working within?

The answer? Limit yourself to only the essential items for your individual business, and produce them *well* with the resources you have.

Your Essential Marketing Materials

The easiest way to throw away your marketing budget is to create and produce marketing materials *you don't need*. Since many pieces of collateral are paper-based, this not only leaves you with boxes of extra (outdated) materials, but also takes a huge toll on the environment.

Take some time to determine what marketing materials you do need, and stick to your list. It's easy to want to "keep up with the Joneses" when your competition comes out with a new piece, but remember your focus should be on attracting and retaining a customer base, not matching the competition item for item.

Know your target market. Make sure you have a solid understanding of your customer base. From that knowledge, you can easily determine what the best way is to reach out and communicate with them. Are they a paper-based or techno savvy client group? Do they appreciate being

11

contacted by email or mail? Are they impressed by flashy design, or simple pieces? *How* you communicate is often just as or more important than *what* you communicate.

Pay attention to costs. Do you really need a die-cut business card? Does your flyer absolutely require ink to the edges? Unique touches to marketing collateral can grab a customer's attention, but they can also dramatically increase the cost of production. Keep an eye out during the design process and make strategic choices about graphic elements.

Make mistakes – in small batches. Not sure if that flyer is going to do the trick? Testing out a limited time offer? Small production runs may cost a little more, but you'll avoid collecting boxes of unusable materials. Or, try a split run with type versions of the same piece and see what works best.

Keep the environment in mind. Environmental responsibility is on everyone's mind these days – including your customers. Always question if a particular marketing item can be produced in electronic format. Consider eliminating plastic bags in exchange for cloth ones, printed with your logo; print everything double-sided; send electronic newsletters; use your website to communicate; and, use recycled paper and envelopes when you can.

Brainstorm your wish list. Create a list of desired marketing materials, and ignore expenses, clients, or any other constraint. Then, beside each item, indicate realistically if it is a needed, wanted, not needed, or electronic item. The next page includes a checklist to get you started. Once you have finished, re-write your list in priority order. This will keep you focused on the essentials only.

To learn the 3 biggest mistakes all business owners make and how to avoid them, visit www.ballistamanagement.com

Marketing Materials Checklist

Item	Need	Want	Don't Need	Electronic
Logo				
Business Cards				
Brochure				
Website				
Newsletter				
Catalogue				
Advertisements				
Flyers				
Fridge Magnet				
Branded Swag (pens, etc.)				
Employee Clothing				
Product Labels				
Signage				
Internal Templates (Fax Cover, Memo, etc.)				
Email Signature				
Blog				
Letterhead + Envelopes				
Thank You Cards				
Notepads				
Seasonal Gifts				
Company Profile				

13

To learn the 3 biggest mistakes all business owners make and how to avoid them, visit www.ballistamanagement.com

Headlines + Sub headlines

If your headlines were all a potential customer read, how do you think your marketing materials would fare? Headlines need to be bold, dramatic, shocking and absolutely answer the questions "What's in it for me?" or, "Why should I care?"

Headlines (and sub headlines) are vital in today's market because we are bombarded with so much information that we scan everything. Readers are skimming your materials to find out why they should bother paying attention to your product or service. Hit their hot buttons, and tell them why they should care, in your headlines!

Remember that headlines and sub headlines are not just for advertisements. They work wonders in newsletters, sales letters, brochures and websites, and can be incorporated into all of your essential marketing materials.

Design

The cost of professional design can eat up the majority of your marketing budget in a hurry. However, the cost of distributing materials that look and feel unprofessional can often be much higher. The key is to find the middle ground.

Unless you have design or desktop publishing experience – or even if you do – your time is probably not best spent designing your own marketing materials. Depending on the size of your business and your graphic needs (i.e.,

To learn the 3 biggest mistakes all business owners make and how to avoid them, visit www.ballistamanagement.com

Do you need frequent photography of your products?) there are a number of options you can choose from:

1. **Hire a design agency.** This is no doubt the most costly of your options. However, if you have a number of items to be designed, you may be able to get a package rate. Another option is to have the design agency create a logo and stationery package for you, then create a "how-to" guide for use of the logo, fonts, and other graphic elements in the rest of your marketing materials.

2. **Hire a freelance designer.** For most small businesses, the benefits of using a freelance designer (aside from cost savings) are convenience and trust. If you are lucky enough to find one you work well with, work hard to establish a seamless working relationship and you'll never worry about the design of your marketing materials again. Ask colleagues for recommendations of local designers, or post an ad on craigslist.

3. **Hire a part-time design employee.** Need to hire someone part-time for a task around the office or shop? Consider recruiting someone with design skills and hiring them for full-time work. This could include graphic design students, or someone with an interest (and talent) in the field.

Whichever option you choose – or if you choose to design your materials yourself - the two most important things to remember about design are:

15

To learn the 3 biggest mistakes all business owners make and how to avoid them, visit www.ballistamanagement.com

1. **Keep it consistent.** Your marketing materials must be consistent, or your customers will never learn to recognize your brand.

2. **Keep it simple.** Simple, clean design is the most effective way of communicating. Use "wow" pieces sparingly.

Guidelines for the Top 10 Marketing Materials

Logo

- **Use design resources.** If you are going to spend any money on outside design help, this is the time to do it. Your logo is the visual representation of your product or service, and appears on everything that relates to your business. This is the core of your brand image, and needs to be done right the first time.

- **Remember the purpose.** The logo needs to be a unique reflection of your business, your business values, and the industry you work in. Before you commit to your logo, make sure to give careful consideration to color choice, image selection and image recognition – as well as the logos that already exist in the marketplace. Test it out on your family and friends for an outside opinion and use their feedback.

- **Don't get too complicated.** Can it be produced (and seen clearly) in black and white? In a single color? With your company name? Too often businesses design their own logos that include a complex assortment of photos, words, and solid design elements. These do not

16

photocopy well, and can't be clearly read at a small scale. Keep your logo design down to a graphic image and the name of your business.

Business cards

- **Cover the basics**. A business card needs to communicate your basic contact information to potential clients, including who you are and *what your business does*. Make sure you've covered the basics and made it easy for them to be in touch.

  o **Name**
  o **Title**
  o **Company Name**
  o **Company Slogan / Description**
  o **Phone Number**
  o **Email Address**
  o **Fax Number**
  o **Address**
  o **Cell Number (if applicable)**
  o **Website**

- **Make it memorable. Be creative.** Choose interesting shapes, die-cuts, orientation (vertical vs. horizontal), bright colors, and unique materials (wood, plastic, magnet, aluminum or foam). You don't have to go crazy or spend lots of money to do this – simple, clever twists on basic design make an impact. Just keep it relevant to your product or service.

- **Give them a reason to keep it.** What is going to keep them from throwing it out, or filing it in a 3" binder of other cards? Make the card worth keeping by adding something useful to the backside. For example, coffee shops put frequent buyer incentives on the backside

To learn the 3 biggest mistakes all business owners make and how to avoid them, visit www.ballistamanagement.com

of their cards, encouraging customers to keep them in their wallets. Other examples include pick-up schedules, reminders, calendars, testimonials, or coupons.

- **Produce a high quality card.** Use at least 100lb card stock, and print in color. Choose clear, easy to read fonts that aren't any smaller than 9pt.

Letterhead

- **Ensure a professional quality.** Letterhead that is simple, clean, and well produced allows the reader to focus on the important part: the content. Have your letterhead professionally printed on 32lb paper, or choose a textured stock. Show that you are invested in the professionalism of your company.

- **Pay attention to design choices.** The design of your marketing collateral should reflect your corporate values and the personality of your organization. If you are environmentally conscious, choose recycled paper and write it in small print at the bottom of the page. Letterhead can also be a place for subtle graphic elements, like watermarks, in addition to your logo.

- **Keep consistent with other materials.** Your letterhead is part of your stationery package, and should look and feel the same as the rest of your pieces. For example, if your business cards have been printed with rounded corners, so should your letterhead. Use consistent fonts, colors, and logo placement on your letterhead, business cards, fax

To learn the 3 biggest mistakes all business owners make and how to avoid them, visit www.ballistamanagement.com

cover sheets, and other internal documents to ensure recognition and ease of readability.

Brochures

- **Cover the basics.** Each brochure you produce should include your basic marketing message, USP, and detailed company contact information. Product or service features, and customer benefits should be clearly displayed and described.

- **Be purpose-focused.** Why are you producing this brochure? Are you featuring a new product line? Trying to increase awareness? Introducing your service to a new market? Stay closely connected to the purpose behind your brochure, and ensure that all of the information (and images) in the brochure support that purpose.

- **Keep it simple.** Make sure the design and information organization is clean and easy to navigate. Like advertisements, leaving blank spaces gives the reader a break and makes it easier to narrow in on key messages.

- **Choose high quality production.** If you don't invest in your business, why should anyone else? Produce your brochure on high quality paper, in vivid color, and have it professionally folded. An impressive-looking brochure will travel farther than a homemade one – from one client's hands to another's.

- **Keep it fresh.** If you produce brochures on a regular basis, consider giving each a theme to distinguish the information as new and

To learn the 3 biggest mistakes all business owners make and how to avoid them, visit www.ballistamanagement.com

interesting. Keep the overall look and feel consistent, but play with images and content layout to revitalize the design.

Newsletters

- **Be in touch.** Don't wait until your existing clients walk back into your store. Show them they're important to your business, and keep them updated on new products and services by keeping distributing a personalized newsletter.

- **Use an online distribution service.** Online email marketing tools (CRM tools) have never been easier or cheaper to use, and enable you to personalize your letters without much effort. They will also track for you which clients open their newsletters, and which click through to your website.

- **Provide information, tell a story.** Engage the reader with a short anecdote, or a piece of relevant information. Many people are bombarded by hard-copy and electronic letters on a daily basis, so make sure yours is worthy of their reading time. Include an "experts corner" or "new product feature" and structure the newsletter like your own business newspaper. Add links to relevant media articles, or special offers.

- **Choose a frequency you can maintain.** Newsletters can be time consuming, so be realistic about how often you promise to distribute them. This depends on your resources, and the needs of your business,

To learn the 3 biggest mistakes all business owners make and how to avoid them, visit www.ballistamanagement.com

but generally once a month to once every three months is a good time frame.

Company (or Corporate) Profile

- **Your ultimate company brochure.** Your company profile includes all pertinent information on your business and your offering, and acts as the base for all other marketing items. These are generally longer pieces – from five to 20 pages in length, allowing you ample room for written and visual content.

- **Tell your story.** The company profile is the place to tell the story of your business. Engage the reader, use anecdotes, and describe how and why your company was created. If you inherited the family business, describe how you're carrying on tradition and instilling new life. If you created your company from scratch with your college roommate, let the reader know. These real life details are interesting and establish trust with your potential clients and associates.

- **Communicate your values.** Here you have the space to describe your company's vision, values and approach, or philosophies. Make sure you relate your values to your offering, and keep this section short and succinct.

- **Explain your offering – features, benefits and all.** Just like your brochure, make sure to describe the full features and benefits of your product or service. Sprinkle testimonials throughout the design to back up your statements. This can include your full range of services,

21

or simply an overview of your product types. Use professional images and creative copy to keep readers engaged.

- **Choose high-quality design and production.** Spend time creating a company profile that will last. Then, spend money producing one that will impress. Choose glossy paper, and a high-quality press, and leave the profiles around your store and office for clients to read and admire.

Signage

- **Get professional advice.** Outdoor signage can be a daunting task for anyone who hasn't designed, produced, or otherwise gone through the process. Since signage is influenced by a variety of factors – one of which is your municipal government signage bylaw – you may wish to enlist the help of a professional (a signage designer or printer) to guide you through the process and avoid costly errors.

- **Make it visible.** All of your outdoor signage should be easily seen from the street, or within the plaza or complex you are located in. In some cases, you may need more than one sign to do this. Keep in mind how your sign will look at night, as well as during the day, as your company logo and phone number or website needs to be visible at all times.

- **Make it distinct.** When it comes to signage, you can get really creative with materials, lights, and colors. While you need to maintain logo, color, and font consistency, you can add other graphic elements

To learn the 3 biggest mistakes all business owners make and how to avoid them, visit www.ballistamanagement.com

that may not work on the rest of your collateral, including 3D elements and window treatments. Make it memorable.

- **Remember your indoor signage.** Every business needs indoor signage to continually remind customers where they are. This includes section signage, product signage, way finding systems, and promotion announcements. If your business is located in an office, consider signage with your logo and company name above the reception area. Again, keep this signage consistent with the rest of your company materials, and you will be contributing to brand recognition.

Advertisements + Flyers

- **Place ads strategically.** Once you have determined who your target market is, you need to focus on advertising in the publications they are most likely to read, and distributing flyers in places they are most likely to be. Spend ad dollars strategically, and don't spend them all at once. Take time to test what publications work, and which don't by measuring the response from each placement. And, when you place ads, request placement that is well-forward and in the top right hand corner.

- **Grab their attention.** You have less than half a second to grab the attention of your audience with print advertising, so use it wisely. Spend the bulk of your time crafting the headline and choosing compelling images.

To learn the 3 biggest mistakes all business owners make and how to avoid them, visit www.ballistamanagement.com

- **Keep their attention.** If you caught their attention, you have another two seconds to keep it. Use subheadings to further entice them to read on for the details of your product or service offer.

- **Tell them why they should buy.** Always include your marketing message or USP in your advertising. Describe the features and benefits of your product or service, but focus on the benefits that will trigger an emotional response from your target audience – love, money, luxury, convenience, and security.

- **Tell them how they can buy.** Include a call to action beside your contact information, and include your phone number, website address, and business address (if applicable). You may wish to include a scarcity or urgency offer to compel your readers to act fast.

- **Know the importance of white space.** If you try to cram too much information into your ad or flyer, your readers will skip it. Clean, clear, easy to read ads and one-page flyers with succinct messages are most effective.

Website

- **Be purpose-focused.** Like your brochure, your website can serve a number of purposes. To be effective, you need to narrow in on the specific purpose when designing the content structure of the pages. Who is your audience? What do you want them to leave the site knowing? What do you want the site to make them do? Visit your

To learn the 3 biggest mistakes all business owners make and how to avoid them, visit www.ballistamanagement.com

store? Buy your offering? Pick up the phone? Make sure you are clear on this point before you start.

- **Make the address easy to remember (and find!).** A website address that is too long or too complicated will not get remembered, or found. Do a search for available website addresses that relate to your business or marketing message, and try to secure a site with a .com ending. If your company name is taken, use your USP or guarantee instead.

- **Focus on content.** The overall structure of how you organize the content on your site is like the foundation of your house. You can change the paint color, and the furniture, but the foundation is more or less there for good. Before you work with a designer and create the visual fabric of your website, focus on creating solid copy that is clearly organized. Put together a map of your structure, starting with your homepage and subpages, and allocating specific content to each page.

- **Revitalize regularly.** Your company is always changing, and so should your website. This is an important (and relatively inexpensive) way to communicate your company news and achievements, and most likely the easiest accessed source of information. Have areas for easy content updates – like a "news" section – and make sure sections like "employees" and "services" are kept up to date. For larger updates, go back to your purpose and website map, and make sure the content changes still support the original intent of the website.

To learn the 3 biggest mistakes all business owners make and how to avoid them, visit www.ballistamanagement.com

- **Organize for intuition.** Make key information easy to access – especially your contact information. You can quickly tell if a website is easy to navigate, because the information you are looking for appears in a natural order. For example, when visiting a restaurant website, a link to the reservations page is provided on the menu page. While you're putting together your website map, do some research online and investigate what does and doesn't work. A good rule of thumb is to ensure it takes no more than three clicks to access a page. Bury content too deep, and your audience will get frustrated and leave.

- **Keep consistent with marketing materials.** Your website is an extension of your marketing campaign, and should be treated as such. Use consistent logo placements, fonts, colors and images so that all elements of your collateral are unified. Likewise with marketing campaigns. If you are running a new promotion, or featuring a new item in an advertisement, include that information on your website. Customers responding to the ad will be reinforced, and customers who did not see the ad will be aware of the offer.

- **Measure your results.** Your website is a piece of your marketing collateral, just like brochures and advertisements, and should be evaluated for effectiveness on a regular basis. Easy website analysis tools, like Google Analytics, will show you which pages your audience is viewing, how long they're staying on each page, and where and when they leave the site. That is powerful information when it comes to structuring content, and choosing which page to put your most important messages.

To learn the 3 biggest mistakes all business owners make and how to avoid them, visit www.ballistamanagement.com

Final thoughts

This chapter can be summed up with: create a brand and ensure that brand is the image you portray to your prospects, no matter the medium. Your brand is synonymous with your company. As you create a marketing plan, your brand should be ever present throughout.

Client Testimonial

"When I first came to Adolfo, I thought I had my marketing set up and ready to go. Our first meeting was very eye opening because everything I thought I was doing right, was proven wrong. My marketing was all over the place, without a concise message of who I was. Once we shored up my brand and developed the right logo and message, the flow of clients was greater than I expected! It truly is amazing how a couple of tweaks can make such a huge difference!"

~K. P.

To learn the 3 biggest mistakes all business owners make and how to avoid them, visit www.ballistamanagement.com

3

How to Profit through Time Management

Manage Time Like Money

Why did you get into business for yourself? Was it to be your own boss? Choose your own hours? Have more time with the family? Spend more time doing what you love? Chances are, you answered yes to all these questions.

These days, you probably wonder where the time went. Why you spent 12 hours at work and barely make a dent in your to-do list. We already know that time is a key resource for you and your business, but it's also a key resource in your life. Harnessing and leveraging time is the only way to enjoy life, and have a profitable business at the same time.

Most business owners carefully manage their financial and personnel resources, and pay due attention to their performance. Marketing plans and budgets are created, people are hired and fired. What most business owners don't realize is that time – and the time of all employees – requires the same attention and diligent management.

Time will never manage itself. The decision to make a pro-active effort to manage your time must come from you. Once you have committed

To learn the 3 biggest mistakes all business owners make and how to avoid them, visit www.ballistamanagement.com

to taking ownership for your own time management, there are a host of tools available to you. But first, you must understand how much your time is actually worth, and where you are currently spending it.

What is Your Time Worth?

Ever wonder what your time is actually worth? Here's a quick way to figure it out:

Target annual income	A.
Working days in a year	B. 235
Working hours in a day	C. 7
Working hours in a year	D. 1,645
A ÷ D = YOUR HOURLY WORTH (before tax + expenses)	E.

This is a very simple calculation intended to put your time in perspective. In reality, no one is productive for each of the 1,645 hours. Various studies have put actual productivity at anywhere between 25 minutes and four hours per day. Either way, there's a lot of room for improvement.

Let's look at it another way:

Your age	A.
Days in a year	B.
Days spent on earth to date (A x B)	C.
Average life expectancy	D. 70
Total projected days on earth (D x B)	E.
Estimated days left (E – C)	F.

To learn the 3 biggest mistakes all business owners make and how to avoid them, visit www.ballistamanagement.com

This exercise isn't intended to scare you, but bring your attention to the importance of choosing how you spend each hour you have available. It is a choice! By developing the skills required to manage your time, you will not only have a profitable business, but a rewarding and balanced life.

The Five Culprits of Time Theft

Chances are – if you're like most people – you have no idea where your time goes. You're likely frustrated by the fact that you can spend 10, 12, even 14 hours a day working, and not make a dent in your to-do list, or only bill half of those hours.

When we're too busy and overloaded with work, we often switch into reactive mode. We can't make it to the bottom of the pile, and end up handling issues and making decisions at the last minute. One of the great benefits of choosing to become proactive in time management is that you can become proactive in all other areas of your business. When in proactive mode, you can take steps to grow your business through networking, building programs, and establishing systems.

Before you investigate where your time goes, let's take a look at the top five culprits of modern-day time theft:

1. Your Email

How many times a day do you check your email? Is Outlook or Mail constantly running on your desktop? Email – internal, external, personal and business   clogs up your day like no other communication channel. For many

30

of us, it is possible to spend the entire day writing and responding to emails without even glancing at our inbox. The number of emails sent and received each day by the average person in 2007 was 147. Multiply that by an average of two minutes per message, and you have spent almost five hours one email in a single day.

2. Your Cell Phone (Or Blackberry)

Cell phones have created convenience, security, and the luxury of telecommuting – but they don't call it a Blackberry for nothing. PDAs and cell phones have also created a society that expects to be able to reach you at any moment, or at least receive instant responses to their calls. Your cell phone or PDA not only robs you of your time during the day, but also during the evenings, and on weekends when you are not at work.

3. Your Open Door Policy

If you make it easy for your staff and associates to interrupt you, they will. Too often, open-door policies are set up by human resource departments to create clear communication channels. Instead, they create a clog of employees lined up at your door seeking immediate answers to non-emergent issues.

4. Meetings

How many times have you been to a meeting that was scheduled to be an hour, and ended up lasting three? How often do you attend unnecessary meetings? Or meetings that run off-topic? Meetings can be a huge source of wasted time – your valuable time. In a senior management or ownership

31

position, your day may consist of back-to-back meetings, leaving only your evening hours to complete the tasks that should have been done during the day.

5. YOU!

Every person has daily habits that sabotage their ability to work productively and efficiently. Many entrepreneurs and business owners can't separate business hours from leisure hours. Some get caught in a time warp while surfing the internet. Others - mainly overachievers – can become paralyzed by perfectionism or procrastination. Mainly we just don't have the tools to schedule and structure our time in a way that fits with our working style.

Where Does Your Time Go?

So far we've seen that time is a resource that should be as carefully managed as cash, we've figured out what your time is worth, and looked at the top five culprits of time theft. You've committed to taking steps to become a better time manager. What now?

Personal Time Management Research Exercise

The next step is to take a good, (and honest!) look at how you spend your time. Once you understand your patterns and habits, you begin to implement the strategies in this chapter that will make you a better time manager.

Here is the three step process to ensure you are making the best use of your time.

To learn the 3 biggest mistakes all business owners make and how to avoid them, visit www.ballistamanagement.com

Step One: Time Audit

Use the Time Log Worksheet at the back of this chapter to record how you spend your time for three working days in a row. Be honest, and be specific. Include time spent in transit, surfing the web, interacting with clients and colleagues, as well as how your time is spent at home in the evenings. The more information you can record, the easier it will be to analyze your time management skills in step two.

Step Two: Time Categorization

Once you have recorded your time for three days, sit down with all three sheets in front of you and identify the following using different colored markers or highlighters:

- Driving, public transportation or other travel
- Eating, including food preparation
- Personal Errands
- Exercise
- Watching TV
- Sleeping, including naps
- Using the computer, personal use only
- Being with family / friends
- Emailing, including checking, reading, and returning messages
- Talking on the phone, including checking and returning messages
- Internal meetings
- External meetings
- Administrative work
- Client work
- Non-client, non-administrative work

33

Step Three: Time Analysis

Now that you have identified how you have spent your time, go through the worksheets one more time and identify if you have spent enough, too much, or too little time on each main task.

Then, based on your observations, answer the following questions:

1. What patterns do you notice about how you spend your time during the day? (i.e., When are you most productive? Least productive? Most or least interrupted?)

_____

_____

_____

_____

2. Write down the four highest priorities in your life right now. Does your timesheet reflect these priorities?

_____

_____

_____

_____

To learn the 3 biggest mistakes all business owners make and how to avoid them, visit www.ballistamanagement.com

3. If you have more time, what would you do?

_____

_____

_____

_____

4. If you had less time, what wouldn't you do?

_____

_____

_____

_____

5. Could you remove the items in question four and add the items in question three? Why or why not?

_____

_____

_____

_____

To learn the 3 biggest mistakes all business owners make and how to avoid them, visit www.ballistamanagement.com

6. Is procrastination a problem for you? How much?

_____

_____

_____

_____

Strategies for Profitable Time Management

There are many ways to curb time theft and refine your time management ability. Through a solid understanding of how you currently spend – and waste – time, you can determine which strategies you need to implement to correct unproductive behavior.

Here are 17 ways you can turn **less** of your time into **more** money:

1. Set Clear Priorities

The foundation of time management a clear understanding of what your time is best spent on. Once you accept that you can't do everything, you need to decide what needs to be completed now, what can be completed later, and what someone else can complete. Each to-do list you create should be put through this filter, and reorganized so the highest priority items are on top, and the lowest priority items are less visible, or on the bottom.

To learn the 3 biggest mistakes all business owners make and how to avoid them, visit www.ballistamanagement.com

Once you have established your priorities – which will also naturally reflect the priorities and goals of your business – stick to them. Just because someone else feels something is of a high priority doesn't mean it holds the same status next to your other tasks.

Prioritization is also helpful in your personal life and leisure time. Your spare time is precious – so make sure are clear on how you would like to spend it.

2. Use Your Skills – Delegate Your Weaknesses

As a business owner, your day naturally consists of tasks you dislike doing. Some are essential – signing checks, reviewing financial statements, and other business maintenance – while others are simply not within your skill set.

If you are a strong public speaker, but struggle with report writing – delegate to a copywriter or editor. If you own a retail store and have no experience in design – outsource your signage. These freelance professionals often cost half as much as you, and take half as long to complete the task. Your time is saved for tasks that use and strengthen your skills effectively, your stress is managed, and ultimately a better product is produced.

3. Delegate, Delegate, Delegate

As a small business owner, the only way you will ever get everything done is by delegating. Delegation is a vital skill that needs to be refined and practiced, and once mastered is the key to profitable time management.

To learn the 3 biggest mistakes all business owners make and how to avoid them, visit www.ballistamanagement.com

Too often, owners and managers believe that it will be "faster" or "more efficient" to complete the task themselves than to train and monitor someone else. Other times, there are no internal resources to download assignments to.

As a result, the following trends can be seen in many small companies:

- Owners and senior staff are stressed and overworked, while junior staff are underutilized and under capacity.

- Staff members are not given an opportunity to grow and develop in their roles, and may perceive a lack of trust or confidence in their ability. The company loses good people.

- Owners and senior staff are always in a reactive state, instead of a visionary or proactive state.

- Delegation happens at the very last minute, and junior staff has little understanding of either the overall project or expectations for the task.

The easiest way to fix this problem is before it starts. Create a solid team of staff members around you who are well-trained and prepared to support the business. Attract and retain qualified and quality people who can be cross-trained and promoted within the company. Ensure that communication flows throughout the business, so everyone has the product and service knowledge to step in and assist when necessary.

38

4. Learn to Say "No"

It's easy to fall into the habit of saying yes to everything. You are, after all the business owner, right? No one can complete these tasks as well as you, right? You'll lose that customer if you don't help them with their garage sale, right?

Wrong. The most successful business owners have a keen understanding of how their time is best spent, and *delegate* the remaining responsibilities to trusted others. It's too easy to say yes to every request in the moment, and later feel overwhelmed when it's added to your to do list. You may not ruffle any feathers, but what toll does it take on your stress level? Your workload? Your time is valuable – so protect it!

Remember that if it is too challenging to say no immediately, you can always request some time to think about it. This way, you can evaluate your workload and realistically decide whether or not you can take on a new project. Then, stand by your decision, or assist in bringing in the necessary resources to get it done.

5. Create (and keep!) a Strict Schedule

While multi-tasking is a desirable skill, it is also often a time thief. Attempting to do too many things at one time ensures that nothing gets done. As a business owner, you need to be able to focus and concentrate on essential projects without interruptions.

The only way to do this is the commit to a strict schedule. Once you understand your work style and concentration patterns, you can allocate

39

To learn the 3 biggest mistakes all business owners make and how to avoid them, visit www.ballistamanagement.com

periods of the day to specific tasks. This includes personal and leisure time – schedule it, and stick to it.

Schedule time for: list-creation + prioritization, email messages, telephone messages, internal meetings, client meetings, meeting preparation, "me-time", family time, recreation + fitness, daily business tasks, and blocks for focused work.

Remember that there is a training period involved in beginning a new routine – for yourself and those around you. Use your voicemail, out-of-office email message, and a closed door to begin to let people know when you will not be disturbed.

6. Make Decisions

The choice to not make a decision is a decision in itself. The most successful business owners have the ability to make good decisions quickly and efficiently, and do not waste time deliberating over simple choices.

In leadership positions, often people are afraid of making the wrong decision or looking foolish if they make a mistake in front of junior staff. What they don't realize, is that hesitating or avoiding decision making impacts their leadership just as much or more than making the wrong decision. Not only can being indecisive be personally stressful, but it is also stressful for those around you whose tasks are waiting on your choices.

Remember, you must make the best decision with the information you have, in the time frame you have to make the decision. No one expects you to be a fortune teller – be decisive, make some mistakes, and learn from them.

To learn the 3 biggest mistakes all business owners make and how to avoid them, visit www.ballistamanagement.com

7. Manage Telephone Interruptions

This is a huge source of time theft that can easily be managed and avoided. If you are available to take phone calls at any time of day, you are setting yourself up to take work home in the evenings. The phone will always ring when you are focused on an important task, and this is something can easily be avoided.

Figure out when you are most productive. Is it in the morning or the afternoon? Before, during, or after lunch? Once you have identified this time period, set your phone on "do not disturb" or have your calls directed to voicemail. If you do not have a receptionist, a variety of automatic answering systems are available for a nominal fee. To structure your phone time further, let callers know on your voicemail what specific time of day is best to reach you via phone. Then, set that time aside to receive and return phone calls.

8. Keep Your Work Environment Organized

Have you ever tried to make dinner in a messy kitchen? More of your time is spent looking for (and cleaning) dishes and tools than actually spent cooking the meal.

The same goes for your work environment. If your desk and office is in a constant state of chaos, then you mind will be too. In fact, some studies have revealed that the average senior business leader spends nearly four weeks each year navigating through messy or cluttered desks, looking for lost information. Does that sound like productive time to you?

To learn the 3 biggest mistakes all business owners make and how to avoid them, visit www.ballistamanagement.com

Once you make the initial clean sweep, it's easy to maintain order in the chaos:

- Tidy your desk at the beginning and end of each day. Attach pertinent documents to your to do list, or have clear and organized folders for loose papers.

- Organize your supplies drawer so you have easy access to stationery like pens, post-it notes, staplers and highlighters. Every minute counts!

- Only have the documents and files you are working on, on your desk. The rest should be neatly filed on a side table for later retrieval.

- Keep personal items (like photos or memorabilia) out of your primary line of vision. These can be distracting and encourage daydreaming.

As for your office or store, there are many ways to make its layout more conducive to effective time management. Try:

- Minimizing the distance between the reception desk and electronics like photocopies and fax machines.

- Keep a clear line of sight between your office and the most productive area of your business, so you are aware of what is happening amongst your staff.

- Organize shelves and filling cabinets so files are not only easily accessed, but out of sight when not being used. Consider putting

To learn the 3 biggest mistakes all business owners make and how to avoid them, visit www.ballistamanagement.com

sliding doors or cabinets in storage areas, and remember that the floor is not a storage cabinet.

9. Keep Your Filing System Organized

If your data isn't organized properly, you will waste hundreds of hours searching for documents you need on a regular basis. This includes both electronic and hard copy files; they need to be organized and up to date.

Customer databases and enquiry records are worth their weight in gold. You can't afford to get behind when updating this information, or poorly store it for later retrieval. There are many easy to use software programs that will manage and organize customer databases for you; it doesn't need to be a time consuming or tedious exercise.

A simple way to manage information is to keep it in short, medium, and long term files for both hard and electronic copies. Create shortcuts on your desktop for folders or files you constantly access. Have short-term files available on your desk, medium-term files available within an arm's reach, and long-term files stored in cabinets.

10. Clearly Communicate – Never Assume

One of the biggest issues for time management in business – and likely the world – is miscommunication. This is a dangerous issue that can cripple any business, including yours. Establishing and enforcing clear policies on things like accurate note taking, task assignments, and phone messages will ensure your staff understand the importance of clear and accurate communication.

To learn the 3 biggest mistakes all business owners make and how to avoid them, visit www.ballistamanagement.com

The easiest habit to start to curb miscommunication is simple: write everything down. Carry a notepad, and jot down key points, figures, agreements and deadlines. Don't assume you'll remember later – you have at least a hundred other things to remember.

Some other simple strategies are:

- Return all communication promptly, including email, letters, faxes and phone calls

- Repeat back phone messages, phone numbers and other figures to confirm you recorded the information correctly.

- Record appointments in your PDA or agenda the moment you make them. Otherwise, you will forget.

- Double check and confirm everything – addresses, phone numbers, meeting locations and times.

- Maintain accurate customer contact logs with dates, times, and phone numbers.

- Post checklists in your store or office for routine operations procedures.

- Announce any changes to the policies and procedures manual immediately.

To learn the 3 biggest mistakes all business owners make and how to avoid them, visit www.ballistamanagement.com

11. Stop Duplicating Efforts

This is a key element of time management that is closely related to effective communication. Studies have continually shown that many businesses often duplicate and triplicate efforts that need only be completed once.

When you have clear systems and procedures in place, your staff will not need to "reinvent the wheel" each time the task needs to be completed. Meeting minutes and individual task assignments will ensure everyone is on the same page and understands their personal responsibilities.

Simple examples of this include re-reading your to-do list each hour to determine what the next important item is. If your list is already structured by priority, this is a needless task. If two staff members are working on similar projects, but unaware of the other, the work will not only be inconsistent, but the efforts will be duplicated. These are easy problems to fix, once they have been identified and communicated.

12. Say Goodbye to Procrastination + Perfectionism

Procrastination is something we all face at one time or another – and likely have since our school days. However, given the pace that the world operates at today, you will only fall behind your competitor if you allow procrastination to rule your day. So how you do avoid it? It's simple. Stop, and just get started, no matter how boring, tedious, or painful the project may be. Reward yourself by crossing each step off your to-do list.

To learn the 3 biggest mistakes all business owners make and how to avoid them, visit www.ballistamanagement.com

Many small business owners also fall victim to perfectionism, which can be paralyzing. The fear that there isn't enough time or resources to "get it perfect" will sometimes stop you dead in your tracks. Perfectionism can also hinder your ability to delegate and say no to tasks you believe no one else can complete "better". Do the best you can with the time and resources you have – and just get started.

13. Plan Your Work, Work Your Plan

Have you ever placed an advertisement on the fly because it was "cheaper", "faster", or "more urgent" than creating a marketing plan? Do you and your staff have a clear idea of where your business is headed over the next six to 12 months, or five years?

Many studies show that less than 10% of small businesses have up to date marketing and business plans, as compared to the majority of large corporations and public companies, which have both.

Marketing and business plans take time and effort to create – but they work, and pay off in spades. They also save you time and money as compared to a haphazard or fly-by-the-seat-of-your-pants strategy. With a marketing plan in place, you will have an idea of how many ads you will be placing in a year, which will earn you a volume discount. Your marketing materials will complement each other, and deliver the same message to the same target audience. Designers will charge less for a package of collateral than for individual collateral items.

To learn the 3 biggest mistakes all business owners make and how to avoid them, visit www.ballistamanagement.com

A business plan will provide you with a guide to reference when making decisions. You can repeatedly ask if the endeavor at hand will contribute to your overall vision, or just seems like a good idea or price.

Remember that planning includes both short and long-term time frames, and applies to both your daily to-do list, and your marketing budget. It provides you with a means to measure your progress, assists in identifying priorities, and helps to manage your time.

14. Avoid Needless, Impromptu + Unstructured Meetings

This may seem like a time theft issue that is out of your control, but it's not. You are in control of your own time, and through strict scheduling can establish a structure for internal and external meetings that everyone around you can work within.

Minimize impromptu internal meetings by letting your staff know when you're available for a "quick chat" and when you are not. If it is important, ask them to schedule a time to meet with you that works with both of your schedules. This not only saves you time, but encourages staff to find solutions to their own issues, and only approach you with more urgent or challenging matters.

You can't avoid having meetings, but you can avoid having unstructured meetings. Ask for or create an agenda for each meeting you attend, with a clear objective and an amount of time allocated to each item. This will keep your meetings focused and on task. If a meeting does run late, give yourself a reasonable buffer, and politely leave for your next appointment.

To learn the 3 biggest mistakes all business owners make and how to avoid them, visit www.ballistamanagement.com

You can always follow up with a colleague to catch-up on the pertinent items you may have missed.

15. Establish Clear Policies + Procedures

A clear policy and procedures manual is like a marketing or business plan – it takes time to create, but ultimately saves everyone in your company time, money and effort. A step-by-step guide to "the way we do things here" is an invaluable resource for your existing and new staff, and provides clear expectations for how you like things done.

Too many businesses make up policies and procedures on the fly – creating dangerous scenarios where mistakes are made and expectations are not clear. Some items that should be included in a comprehensive policy and procedures manual include:

- Recruitment
- Customer relations
- Customer enquiries
- Customer complaints
- Returns
- Exchanges

- Late Payments
- Salary structure
- Bonus structure
- Employee review
- Theft
- Harassment

16. Keep the Right Set of Tools

The equipment your business needs to operate (and grow!) effectively should always be on hand, or easily contracted out. This is specific to each company, and closely related to costs – including the cost of your time.

To learn the 3 biggest mistakes all business owners make and how to avoid them, visit www.ballistamanagement.com

Whether you are a high-tech business or local retailer, knowledge of the latest advancements in technology will increase your efficiency. It will help you stay on top of the competitor, maintain your position as an expert, and perhaps provide an easier way of getting things done.

Always ask yourself if these purchases are essential to your business –could perhaps make these purchases from a second hand dealer to minimize cost? Is it more cost effective to outsource or sub-contract the tasks to someone with access to this equipment, or to buy the equipment yourself?

If your business relies on tools and technology for daily tasks (such as the trades' profession) then obtaining the best quality you can afford is crucial.

17. Maintain Your Equipment

This may seem obvious, but you'll understand the importance if your network server has ever crashed, or point of sale system has malfunctioned. Your business can be slowed to a stand-still if your equipment is not in good working order. Of course there are instances that can't be predicted, but regular maintenance of your essential equipment will reduce these occurrences and help to anticipate when old equipment needs to be repaired or replaced.

Personal Time Management Strategy

Choose the top five tips from this chapter that you think will help you the most, given your personal time management research. Write them below, with three corresponding actions that you will start tomorrow. For example, if you are going to set a strict schedule, three actions might be to establish the schedule, communicate it to your staff, and re-record your voicemail message.

To learn the 3 biggest mistakes all business owners make and how to avoid them, visit www.ballistamanagement.com

1._____

     a._____

     b._____

     c._____

2._____

     a._____

     b._____

     c._____

3._____

     a._____

     b._____

     c._____

To learn the 3 biggest mistakes all business owners make and how to avoid them, visit www.ballistamanagement.com

4._____

    a._____

    b._____

    c._____

5._____

    a._____

    b._____

    c._____

Final thoughts

This chapter is very personal to me. All of the strategies mentioned here I personally use. They helped me increase my productivity while also increasing my satisfaction with life. These techniques allowed me to work full time, while pursuing my college degree, and still spend quality time with my family. Time is our most precious resource. Understanding how to master time will truly change your life and up your success in ways you never thought possible.

Timesheet | Day One

Timeslot	Activities	More/Less/ Enough time?
7:00 – 7:30		
7:30 – 8:00		
8:00 – 8:30		
8:30 – 9:00		
9:00 – 9:30		
10:00 – 10:30		
10:30 – 11:00		
11:00 – 11:30		
11:30 – 12:00		
12:00 – 12:30		
12:30 – 1:00		
1:00 – 1:30		
1:30 – 2:00		
2:00 – 2:30		
2:30 – 3:00		
3:00 – 3:30		
3:30 – 4:00		
4:00 – 4:30		
4:30 – 5:00		
5:00 – 5:30		
5:30 – 6:00		
6:00 – 10:00 (Evening)		

To learn the 3 biggest mistakes all business owners make and how to avoid them, visit www.ballistamanagement.com

Timesheet | Day Two

Timeslot	Activities	More/Less/ Enough time?
7:00 – 7:30		
7:30 – 8:00		
8:00 – 8:30		
8:30 – 9:00		
9:00 – 9:30		
10:00 – 10:30		
10:30 – 11:00		
11:00 – 11:30		
11:30 – 12:00		
12:00 – 12:30		
12:30 – 1:00		
1:00 – 1:30		
1:30 – 2:00		
2:00 – 2:30		
2:30 – 3:00		
3:00 – 3:30		
3:30 – 4:00		
4:00 – 4:30		
4:30 – 5:00		
5:00 – 5:30		
5:30 – 6:00		
6:00 – 10:00 (Evening)		

To learn the 3 biggest mistakes all business owners make and how to avoid them, visit www.ballistamanagement.com

Timesheet | Day Three

Timeslot	Activities	More/Less/ Enough time?
7:00 – 7:30		
7:30 – 8:00		
8:00 – 8:30		
8:30 – 9:00		
9:00 – 9:30		
10:00 – 10:30		
10:30 – 11:00		
11:00 – 11:30		
11:30 – 12:00		
12:00 – 12:30		
12:30 – 1:00		
1:00 – 1:30		
1:30 – 2:00		
2:00 – 2:30		
2:30 – 3:00		
3:00 – 3:30		
3:30 – 4:00		
4:00 – 4:30		
4:30 – 5:00		
5:00 – 5:30		
5:30 – 6:00		
6:00 – 10:00 (Evening)		

To learn the 3 biggest mistakes all business owners make and how to avoid them, visit www.ballistamanagement.com

Daily To-Do List | Business

Task	Priority (1-10)	Deadline?	Delegation?

To learn the 3 biggest mistakes all business owners make and how to avoid them, visit www.ballistamanagement.com

Weekly To-Do List | Personal (Family, Leisure, etc.)

Task	Priority (1-10)	Deadline?	Delegation?

To learn the 3 biggest mistakes all business owners make and how to avoid them, visit www.ballistamanagement.com

4

Generating an Unlimited Amount

of Leads for Your Business

Where do your customers come from?

Most people would probably choose advertising as an answer. Or referrals. Or direct mail campaigns. This may seem true, but it's not really accurate.

Your customers come from leads that have been turned into sales. Each customer goes through a two-step process before they arrive with their wallets open. They have been converted from a member of a target market, to a lead, then to a customer.

So, would it not stand to reason then, that when you advertise or send any marketing material out to your target market, that you're not really trying to generate customers? That instead, you're trying to generate leads.

To learn the 3 biggest mistakes all business owners make and how to avoid them, visit www.ballistamanagement.com

When you look at your marketing campaign from this perspective, the idea of generating leads as compared to customers seems a lot less daunting. The pressure of closing sales is no longer placed on advertisements or brochures.

From this perspective then, the **general purpose of your advertising and marketing efforts is to generate leads from qualified customers.** Seems easy enough, doesn't it?

Where Are Your Leads Coming From?

If I asked you to tell me the top three ways you generate new sales leads, what would you say?

- Advertising?
- Word of mouth?
- Networking?
- …don't know?

The first step toward increasing your leads is in understanding how many leads you currently get on a regular basis, as well as where they come from. Otherwise, how will you know when you're getting more phone calls or walk-in customers?

If you don't know where your leads come from, start *today.* Start asking every customer that comes through your door, "how did you hear about us?" or "what brought you in today?" Ask every customer that calls where they found your telephone number, or email address. Then, *record the information for at least an entire week.*

58

To learn the 3 biggest mistakes all business owners make and how to avoid them, visit www.ballistamanagement.com

When you're finished, take a look at your spreadsheet and write your top three lead generators here:

1. _____

2. _____

3. _____

From Lead to Customer: Conversion Rates

Leads mean nothing to your business unless you convert them into customers. You could get hundreds of leads from a single advertisement, but unless those leads result in purchases, it's been a largely unsuccessful (and costly) campaign.

The ratio of leads (potential customers) to transactions (actual customers) is called your conversion rate. Simply divide the number of customers who actually purchased something by the number of customers who inquired about your product or service, and multiply by 100.

# of transactions / # of leads x 100 = % conversion rate

If, in a given week, I have 879 customers come into my store, and 143 of them purchase something, the formula would look like this:

[143 (customers) / 879 (leads)] x 100 = 16.25% conversion rate

What's Your Conversion Rate?

To learn the 3 biggest mistakes all business owners make and how to avoid them, visit www.ballistamanagement.com

Based on the formula above, you can see that the higher your conversion rate, the more profitable the business.

Your next step is to determine you own current conversion rate. Add up the number of leads you sourced in the last section, and divide that number into the total transactions that took place in the same week.

Write your conversion rate here:

_____.

Quality (or Qualified) Leads

Based on our review of conversion rates, we can see that the number of leads you generate means nothing unless those leads are being converted into customers.

So what affects your ability (and the ability of your team) to turn leads into customers? Do you need to improve your scripts? Your product or service? Find a more competitive edge in the marketplace?

Maybe. But the first step toward increasing conversion rates is to evaluate the leads you are currently generating, and make sure those leads are the right ones.

What are Quality Leads?

Potential customers are potential customers, right? Anyone who walks into your store or picks up the phone to call your business could be convinced to purchase from you, right? Not necessarily, but this is a common assumption most business owners make.

To learn the 3 biggest mistakes all business owners make and how to avoid them, visit www.ballistamanagement.com

Quality leads are the people who are the most likely to buy your product or service. They are the qualified buyers who comprise your target market. Anyone might walk in off the street to browse a furniture store – regardless of whether or not they are in the market for a new couch or bed frame. This lead is solely interested in browsing, and is not likely to be converted to a customer.

A quality lead would be someone looking for a new kitchen table, and who specifically drove to that same furniture because a friend had raved about the service they received that month. **These are the kinds of leads you need to focus on generating.**

How Do You Get Quality Leads?

- **Know your target market**. Get a handle on who your customers are – the people who are most likely to buy your product or service. Know their age, sex, income, and purchase motivations. From that information you can determine how best to reach your specific audience.

- **Focus on the 80/20 rule.** A common statistic in business is that 80% of your revenue comes from 20% of your customers. These are your star clients, or your ideal clients. These are the clients you should focus your efforts on recruiting. This is the easiest way to grow your business and your income.

- **Get specific.** Focus not only on who you want to attract, but how you're going to attract them. If you're trying to generate leads from a specific market segment, craft a unique offer to get their attention.

61

- **Be proactive**. Once you've generated a slew of leads, make sure you have the resources to follow up on them. Be diligent and aggressive, and follow up in a timely manner. You've done to work to get them, now reel them in.

Get More Leads from Your Existing Strategies

Increasing your lead generation doesn't necessarily mean diving in and implementing an expensive array of new marketing strategies. Marketing and customer outreach for the purpose of lead generation can be inexpensive, and bring a high return on investment.

You are likely already implementing many of these strategies. With a little tweaking or refinement, you can easily double your leads, and ensure they are more qualified.

Here are some popular ways to generate quality leads:

Direct Mail to Your Ideal Customers

Direct mail is one of the fastest and most effective ways to generate leads that will build your business. It's a simple strategy – in fact, you're probably already reaching out to potential clients through direct mail letters with enticing offers.

The secret to doubling your results is to craft your direct mail campaigns specifically for a highly targeted audience of your *ideal* customers.

Your ideal customers are the people who will buy the most of your products or services. They are the customers who will buy from you over and over again, and refer your business to their friends. They are the group of 20% of your clients who make up 80% of your revenue.

Identify your ideal customers

Who are your ideal customers? What is their age, sex, income, location and purchase motivation? Where do they live? How do they spend their money? Be as specific as possible.

Once you have identified who your ideal customers are, you can begin to determine how you can go about reaching them. Will you mail to households or apartment buildings? Families or retirees? Direct mail lists are available for purchase from a wide range of companies, and can be segregated into a variety of demographic and sociographic categories.

Craft a special offer

Create an offer that's too good to refuse – not for your entire target market, but for your ideal customer. How can you cater to their unique needs and wants? What will be irresistible for them?

For example, if you operate a furniture store, your target market is a broad range of people. However, if you are targeting young families, your offer will be much different than one you may craft for empty-nesters.

Court them for their business

Don't stop at a single mail-out. Sometimes people will throw your letter away two or three times before they are motivated to act. Treat your

To learn the 3 biggest mistakes all business owners make and how to avoid them, visit www.ballistamanagement.com

direct mail campaign like a courtship, and understand that it will happen over time.

First send a letter introducing yourself, and your irresistible offer. Then follow up on a monthly basis with additional letters, newsletters, offers, or flyers. Repetition and reinforcement of your presence is how your customer will go from saying, "who is this company" to "I buy from this company."

Advertise for lead generation

Statistics show that nearly 50% of all purchase decisions are motivated by advertising. It can also be a relatively cost effective way of generating leads.

We've already discussed the importance of ensuring your advertisements are purpose-focused. The general purpose of most advertisements is to increase sales – which starts with leads. However ads that are created solely for lead generation – that is, to get the customers to pick up the phone or walk in the store – are a category of their own.

Lead generation ads are simply designed and create a sense of curiosity or mystery. Often, they feature an almost unbelievable offer. Their purpose is not to convince the customer to buy, but to contact the business for more information.

As always, when you are targeting your ideal audience, you'll need to ensure that your ads are placed prominently in publications that audience reads. This doesn't mean you have to fork over the cash for expensive display

To learn the 3 biggest mistakes all business owners make and how to avoid them, visit www.ballistamanagement.com

ads. Inexpensive advertising in e-mail newsletters, classifieds, and the yellow pages are very effective for lead generation.

Here are some tips for lead generation advertising:

Leverage low-cost advertising

Place ads in the yellow pages, classifieds section, e-mail newsletters, and online. If your target audience is technology savvy, consider new forms of advertising like Facebook and Google Adwords.

Spark curiosity

Don't give them all the information they need to make a decision. Ask them to contact you for the full story, or the complete details of the seemingly outrageous offer.

Grab them with a killer headline

Like all advertising, a compelling headline is essential. Focus on the greatest benefits to the customer, or feature an unbelievable offer.

Referrals and host beneficiary relationships

A referral system is one of the most profitable systems you can create in your business. The beauty is once it's set up, it often runs itself.

Customers that come to you through referrals are often your "ideal customers." They are already trusting and willing to buy. This is one of the most cost-effective methods of generating new business, and is often the most

To learn the 3 biggest mistakes all business owners make and how to avoid them, visit www.ballistamanagement.com

profitable. These referral clients will buy more, faster, and refer further business to your company.

Referrals naturally happen without much effort for reputable businesses, but with a proactive referral strategy you'll certainly double or triple your referrals. Sometimes, you just need to ask!

Here are some easy strategies you can begin to implement today:

Referral incentives

Give your customers a reason to refer business to you. Reward them with discounts, gifts, or free service in exchange for a successful referral.

Referral program

Offer new customers a free product or service to get them in the door. Then, at the end of the transaction, give them three more 'coupons' for the same free product or service that they can give to their friends. Do the same with their friends. This ongoing program will bring you more business than you can imagine.

Host-beneficiary relationships

Forge alliances with non-competitive companies who target your ideal customers. Create cross-promotion and cross-referral direct mail campaigns that benefit both businesses.

To learn the 3 biggest mistakes all business owners make and how to avoid them, visit www.ballistamanagement.com

Lead Management Systems

Once your lead generation strategies are in place, you'll also need a system to manage incoming inquiries. You'll need to ensure you receive enough information from each lead to follow up on at a later date. You'll also need to create a system to organize that information, and track the lead as it is converted into a sale.

Gathering Information from Your Leads

Here is a list of information you should gather from your leads. This list can be customized to the needs of your business, and the type of information you can realistically ask for from your potential customers.

- Company Name
- Name of Contact
- Alternate Contact Person
- Mailing Address
- Phone Number
- Fax Number

- Cell Phone
- Email Address
- Website Address
- Product of Interest
- Other Competitors Engage

Lead List Management Methods:

Once you have gathered information from your lead, you'll need a system to organize their information and keep a detailed contact history.

The simplest way to do this is with a database program, but you can also use a variety of hard copy methods.

To learn the 3 biggest mistakes all business owners make and how to avoid them, visit www.ballistamanagement.com

Electronic Database Programs

- High level of organization available
- Unlimited space for notes and record-keeping
- Data-entry required
- Examples include: MS Outlook, MS Excel, Maximizer
- Customer Relationship Management Software

Index Cards

- Variety of sizes: 3x5, 4X6 or 5X8
- Basic contact information on one side
- Notes on the other side
- Easy to organize and sort

Rolodex System

- Maintain more contacts than index card system
- Easily organized and compact
- Basic contact information on one side
- Notes on the other side
- Can keep phone conversation and purchase details

Notebook

- Best if leads are managed by a single person
- Lots of room for notes
- Inexpensive
- Difficult to re-organize
- Best for smaller lists

To learn the 3 biggest mistakes all business owners make and how to avoid them, visit www.ballistamanagement.com

Business Card Organizer

- Best for small lists – under 100
- Limited space for notes
- No data entry required
- Rolodex-style, or clear binder pages

Final thoughts

Leads are the life blood of any business. One of the first lessons you are taught when you begin a sales role is the importance of your pipeline – the stream of leads that you can contact who have shown interest in your product. Lead generation, then, is of critical importance to a business owner. Without leads, selling is impossible.

Client testimony

"When I started my business, it was because I loved Apps. They were new and I was great at creation. What I was not good at was the sales process. I did not understand lead generation or what it required. I had a great product with little momentum. After Adolfo helped design a lead generation system that fit my personality and my goals, my business took off."

~K.B.

To learn the 3 biggest mistakes all business owners make and how to avoid them, visit www.ballistamanagement.com

5

How to Use Promotions for

Increased Sales Immediately

Promotion and revenue go hand in hand. No matter how long you've been in business, or what kind of company you have; keeping your product/service in the forefront of the consumer's mind is an ongoing process. You want to be the one they remember when they go to buy that hair product or need to get their car fixed.

In simple terms, promotion is about communicating who your company is and enticing your target audience to purchase your product or service. It showcases the marketing messages you put out into the world, and aims to achieve your marketing objectives.

It's an umbrella term that encompasses any activity that is done for the purpose of "getting your name out there" and creating sales. It is one of the main components that make up a marketing plan.

70

Think big shots like Coca Cola and Microsoft no longer have promotional campaigns? On the contrary, in order to stay at the top of their fields they devote a great deal of energy to promotion; and they keep it going regularly.

If you aren't going to the public, but waiting for them to come to you, you're only creating a one way stream of revenue. In this day and age promotion is a cornerstone of success in business.

Why Everyone Needs to Promote Their Business

We've been discussing how essential marketing plans – and proactive strategies in general - are to success in business. Doing so paints the picture of your company's vision. It forces you to ask yourself what your product/service is all about, and how it will meet your target market's need? The groundwork is laid, but how are you going to communicate this with them? This is where promotion comes into the picture....

You can have the best product in the world....but if the world doesn't know about it, it's not doing anyone any good!

"Getting your name out there" is how you are going to create a strong impression in the minds of your potential customers. One way to get into this style of thinking is to see everything you do as a way to do just that. Sure there are standard methods of promotion which can be very useful, but when you "think outside the box" it can really give you an edge against the competition.

The ways of promotion are endless; all you have to do is get yourself into that mind-set. Once you start thinking like the customer, you'll start to

71

To learn the 3 biggest mistakes all business owners make and how to avoid them, visit www.ballistamanagement.com

understand what THEY want, and then the opportunities of how to provide it, as well as how to let them know about it, shine through.

Brand Awareness

In a marketplace that is full of variety for consumers to choose from, maintaining a presence and reputation amongst all the other brands and products is essential. This is a term called brand awareness, which really just means getting your company and its product/service known, by repetitive exposure of your marketing messages and logo to the public. Promotion is what allows you to achieve this. It also creates interest and curiosity around your product/service.

Consistent Promotion

Equally important to promoting yourself in general, is promoting on a consistent basis. The effectiveness of doing it suffers if you don't commit to it on a frequent basis. This doesn't have to cost a lot of money, there are plenty of cost-effective methods to choose from.

The goal is to "touch base" with the public. If they gain some brand awareness and then you disappear for a while they'll forget about you, "out of sight, out of mind". If and when you start putting your promotional communications out there it will take a while to catch on again, and plus it looks inconsistent. And as we all know by this point, the key to success in marketing is consistency!

To learn the 3 biggest mistakes all business owners make and how to avoid them, visit www.ballistamanagement.com

Promotional Strategies

Self-Promotion or Networking

Building relationships is not only the foundation of a success in social situations, but also success in business situations. The two go hand in hand, meaning every situation is a chance to make a potential sale.

Some people feel awkward about showcasing themselves, but no one believes in your product/service more than you do. People sense that genuine enthusiasm and it instills them with confidence. Effective promotion begins with how you promote yourself as an individual.

The key is not to make it the only reason for networking, or at the very least not to let it come across that this is the only reason.

A casual way to create an opportunity to discuss your company is to find out about the other person first. This creates a connection and people are always flattered when you inquire about them. It also gives you the opportunity to learn about their needs and desires. Look for clues of how you could relate your product/service to help them in their life.

When it comes to discussing what "you do for a living" they will be more open to receive your enthusiastic promotion. Even if they don't currently have a need for your product/service they are likely to either keep it in mind for the future, and/or pass that information along to friends and family. This is how you create a buzz, and the beauty of "word of mouth" is born.

73
To learn the 3 biggest mistakes all business owners make and how to avoid them, visit www.ballistamanagement.com

Marketing Promotion

This is used to reach a large number of people simultaneously.

One of the major advantages of using some of these methods is the organic creation of a "brand" for your company. When the messages you are putting out there are consistent, and you provide a product or service of consistent quality, it starts to "make a name" for itself.

For example, Nike doesn't need to write lengthy description of what its products are because they have spent so much effort promoting themselves in the past. Now when you see their little "swoosh" logo, you know which company is being mentioned.

It's pretty hard to achieve that by going door to door talking to your neighbors. Using some of the standard promotion methods to showcase your logo, and expose your company's promotional messages gets you known a whole different level.

Here are some examples of simple and cost-effective promotions:

- **Get your business card into as many hands as possible.** Visit friends and family and leave a small stack of business cards with them to give to others. This can create a tremendous trickle-down effect.

- **Have your company logo professionally painted on your vehicle**

- **Be your own billboard.** Have some shirts printed with you company's info on them and sport one when you're running errands or doing leisure

74

activities. Why not even get a few more made so that friends and family can act as a promo team….free of charge!?

- **Write an article on your area of expertise and submit it to a trade magazine or industry newsletter**. Be sure to include your company's contact information at the bottom.

- **Join a few professional associations and attend meetings and functions as an opportunity to network**

- **Always keep business cards on hand, and give them out throughout the day**

- **Put up flyers on public notice boards/community boards and in related businesses. You can even hand them out on the street!**

Types of Promotions

As previously discussed, you know that promotion is any form of communication regarding your product/service or company. This section discusses the variety of standard promotional methods you can use.

If possible, using a variety of these different types enables you to reach your target market in multiple ways; and since the messages you're putting forward are consistent, this creates a greater impact.

Advertising

This is any form of communication that you pay for. It comes across through another source, but is understood that the message comes from what your company wants the public to know about them.

To learn the 3 biggest mistakes all business owners make and how to avoid them, visit www.ballistamanagement.com

The following outlets are standard methods of advertising:

- Broadcast: Radio, television, internet
- Outdoor: Billboards, bus shelters and even buses themselves
- Print: Programs for event, newspaper/magazines, trade journals

While advertising is projected to the general public, exposing everyone to your message, you want to ensure that you are targeting a specific market. Its effectiveness is easily lost if you are not choosing an outlet that is accepted or used by the group you're selling to. Getting it out there is not enough, it has to make sense.

For example, if you run ads for your new brand of beer on the health and wellness TV station, your sales likely won't be as high as if you aired it during the evenings in between reality TV shows.

Marketing Collateral

This method is often confused with advertising, however it is self-promotion in the fact you don't use any other source to help you get your message across.

Below are commonly used examples:

- Business Cards
- Brochures
- Newsletters
- Flyers
- Posters

To learn the 3 biggest mistakes all business owners make and how to avoid them, visit www.ballistamanagement.com

Public Relations

This is exposure to your company, and/or product/service that comes from a 3rd party – the media. To maintain the legitimacy of the information portrayed in this way you cannot pay for this exposure.

It comes instead by developing positive relationships with people within the media channels. When they understand your company vision, or product potential, you can work together to create communication to the public.

A good way to create a positive image of your company is to sponsor an event which gives back to the community. Then you would want to call up your buddy Jim at the local newspaper or Sally at your town's popular radio station, and chances are they'll help you promote it. It's a nice two way stream because as part of their job they are always looking for stories that will appeal to the public. And now here you are doing something that shows social awareness and involvement.

Traditional Sales

This method of promotion refers to yourself, a member of your sales team, or a retailer communicating about you product/services in a one to one or small group situation.

Examples include:

- Demonstrations/presentations
- Door-to-door
- Telemarketing

To learn the 3 biggest mistakes all business owners make and how to avoid them, visit www.ballistamanagement.com

Sponsorship

This is a way to get exposure by affiliating yourself with another organization. You would offer financial support to this company's event, and in turn they would mention you when promoting their event.

You can use sponsorship in many ways. You can use it to create a positive image, by supporting an event that is important to everyone, e.g. Weekend to End Breast Cancer. Alternatively, it works well when you support a company whose product/service is related to you own, e.g. if you are a shoe company you could sponsor a local 10 km race.

Sales Promotion

Not to be confused with the word promotion itself; sales promotion is the action of offering incentives to entice people to try your product/service. These methods are often used to offer a "taster" of your product or service. They serve as a way of bringing in new clients, who you may not have reached without this bait.

It is also a way of attracting customers from your competitors; who may try your similar product/service because of the low rate, and then be "won over" by the quality of your product/service.

The idea is to make the consumers "an offer they can't refuse".

It is often used for a short time; but if long-term goals are set, and the sales promotion is well planned/ executed with them in mind, it can bring success on this level too.

Use sales promotion(s) in the short-term if you're looking to:

- Match the competition
- Move inventory
- Create cash flow

Use sales promotion(s) in the long-term if you're looking to:

- Create additional revenue or market share
- Increase the size of your target market
- Create a positive experience with the product/service
- Enhance product value and brand power

By this point I'm sure you're dying to know, what are these tools I can use to achieve such great things? Well they are things that we see every day when out in the marketplace. Examples:

1. Coupons – discounted prices are always appealing
2. Gift with purchase offers – to appeal to the "I get more than I'm paying for" mentality
3. Sweepstakes/Contests – you get a chance to win with every purchase
4. Free Samples – there's no risk involved, you know what you're buying
5. Specialties – free gifts used as a reminder items (carry your branding/logo)
6. Rebates – get money back if you mail in form
7. Group Discounts

To learn the 3 biggest mistakes all business owners make and how to avoid them, visit www.ballistamanagement.com

8. Frequent User Incentives – e.g. Get your 7th coffee free after purchasing 6. This is a way to encourage customer loyalty

9. Give-Aways (e.g. Baseball caps or mugs with your logo) – now the public's doing your promoting for you

10. "Early Bird Rates" - this is useful if you are trying to get people to sign up for something, e.g. If you sign-up for this workshop before Oct. 14th the cost is $150.00, after that date it's $180

11. Guarantees – If you're not satisfied with your purchase you can return it for a refund

Packaging

Making sure that the container for your product is appealing, and that it offers the same message as the rest of your promotional efforts is essential. What good is going through all the planning to create a wonderful promotional campaign if a) when the customer gets the product or goes to buy it doesn't draw them in or b) they can't find it because the design fails (e.g. the company or product name is too small or gets lost behind lots of artsy filler).

Customer Service

Now let's say you don't have a product, but a service instead. Even if you are a small business you may have a few employees. It's important that all of the members of your team display a unite front, and communicate the promotion of your service in a consistent manner. And if what your company offers involves these employees providing it for the customer, it is especially important that there is a standard level of service. This is what helps build your brand.

To learn the 3 biggest mistakes all business owners make and how to avoid them, visit www.ballistamanagement.com

Direct Mail

This involves sending out promotional materials addressed to specific individuals. This has become an increasingly popular method of promotion over the last five years.

There are even sources from whom you can buy databases of companies/individuals within your industry, allowing you to send your communication efforts to the people who are the most likely to need your product/services.

Personalizing the promotional materials you send out the response rates increases the "call to action" (specific result you're trying to achieve). The response rates are higher because people by nature are more inquisitive when they see something with their name on it, rather than what may just be perceived as a general flyer.

Trade Shows

Your product or service might be one that is suited to exhibiting at a trade show attended by your target audience. Trade shows are typically one- or two- day events that allow businesses to set up exhibits or booths showcasing their products or capabilities.

Choosing a Strategy

So with all these options, how do you decide which types of promotions will be the most effective, and will give you the most "bang for your buck"?

To learn the 3 biggest mistakes all business owners make and how to avoid them, visit www.ballistamanagement.com

Keep these two things in mind:

Research is crucial. This means studying your target market; as well as the competition. Check out a trade magazine to see how they are marketing similar products/services.

A little creativity can go a long way. Think outside the box, and put your own spin on things. In such an environment that's saturated with so many marketing messages, doing something out of the ordinary will catch consumer attention, make you stand out and give you an edge on the competition.

Planning Your Promotions

Like anything in life, and especially in marketing; a well thought out plan is the starting point from which great successes arise. Just as it is necessary to write a general marketing plan; in order to assess your current situation, where you want to go and what it will look like when you get there; the same must be done to get a clear vision of what you want to achieve from your promotional efforts – your promotional campaign.

What is a promotional plan?

A promotional plan is an outline of the ways you're going to promote your product/service to achieve your marketing goals. The promotional plan is only one component of an overall marketing plan, yet it often gets mistaken however for the marketing plan, as it outlines where most of the marketing budget will go.

To learn the 3 biggest mistakes all business owners make and how to avoid them, visit www.ballistamanagement.com

What do you want to achieve from your promotional efforts?

This is where you would discuss your goals. It is very important to remember that the goals of your promotional efforts are geared to achieve the goals that were set in your marketing plan. Just like the goals in the marketing plan need to focus on achieving the overall objectives of your company.

You want to be as specific as possible here. Just like you don't want to try and be everything to everyone - in terms of your product in the marketplace, you don't want to try and achieve every marketing goal you set at once. Really focus on what you're trying to achieve, whether it be results in the short-term, or paving the way for long-term success. Then just ensure that those are the marketing goals you're working from.

Remember that in order to know whether your efforts have been successful; you have to think in measurable terms from the goal setting phase. By comparing the following two goals it is clear to see which one will be more effective. Goal A = Increase of customers from implementing our new "return business rate". VS Goal B = Increased the repeat customer base by 20%, by year's end, as a result of the newly implemented "return business rate" program.

What message or image do you want to communicate?

You want to make sure that your customers are continually getting the same impression of your product/service, and your company as a whole. To ensure this happens as often as possible, you want to carefully choose what you want to convey.

83

To learn the 3 biggest mistakes all business owners make and how to avoid them, visit www.ballistamanagement.com

Then, make sure all the forms of promotion you take lead back to these core communication messages. This is a similar concept to how your promotional efforts need to correspond with your marketing goals and your marketing goals need to correspond to your company goals.

In our environment we are continually surrounded by messages from different companies. They reach us on deeper levels than we realize. For this reason it is so important to maintain consistency in what and how you are communicating with your target market. The idea is that they get the same message so often that they don't even need to distinguish where or how they got it, it just becomes their association with what you are promoting.

This can only be achieved if you don't have conflicting messages. For example, if your packaging focuses on being environmentally friendly, your advertising campaign is about the great value for money of your product and your press releases discuss the health benefits the consumer is confused. What are you trying to provide me? All these different messages conflict in their minds and they are left felling confused, rather than compelled to buy/try your product.

What tools are you going to use to get your message across and achieve your goals?

The varieties of methods you can use to promote your product/services are limited only by your creativity.

What needs to be done for the plan to come into effect?

This is where you look at logistics. Things to think about:

84

- What kinds of companies will you need to research? (e.g. media, printing, design)
- When does the campaign need to be "up and running?"
- Will all your promotional efforts begin simultaneously, or will they be staggered?
- If you have staff, who will be responsible for what?

How much is it likely to cost to put these promotional efforts in place?

You need to consider how much your promotional vision will cost. And of course, going hand in hand with that is; how much do you have to spend?

One thing to keep in mind is whether or not the need for your product/service changes throughout the year. For example, if you sell snowshoes, this is a seasonal business, and you are not going to need to allot any of your budget toward promoting in the summer.

How will I know if I've achieved my goals? And how will I make sure to keep achieving them?

Having a maintenance plan for monitoring your promotional efforts is a key step; and should not to be overlooked. It ties into the idea of making sure that you're working toward measurable goals. If you don't have a specific result in mind, how do you know when/if you've achieved your goal?

Your maintenance plan should cover at least a full sales cycle for your business. For some, this is seasonal, for others it's annual.

Ways to discover which of your promotional efforts are most effective:

Customers: Your customers are the greatest source you have. After all, your efforts are aimed to appeal to them, so find out which of your promotional activities worked, by asking: "how did you hear about our product/service?" This is the best measure of success you could ask for…and it's free!

Retailers: If you are selling your product via someone else's store, make sure to connect with them regularly to see how things are going. They are an eye-witness to how your product fares against the competition. Find out what they notice in terms of customer perception of your product.

They will also be a different source of feedback than that which comes directly from the customer. They may be privy to information a customer wouldn't tell you, and will likely know all about the praise and/or complaints. So be sure to check in with questions such as: "have they noticed customers picking up your brochures or business cards you left at their store"?

Keep a notebook of comments, feedback and advice from these sources. By referring back to the info you have received by simply seeking this feedback; you can assess which promotional method is bringing in the most sales, and then put more of your efforts and marketing budget toward it in the future.

Promotion Plan Steps

1. Go through the different types of promotional methods and determine their strengths and weaknesses

To learn the 3 biggest mistakes all business owners make and how to avoid them, visit www.ballistamanagement.com

2. Determine the combination of promotion methods you want to implement

3. Decide which of the goals in your marketing plan you want to achieve with your promotional campaign

4. Look at how much money you have in the budget to allot to promotion

5. Decide what percentage of the budget will go to which method of promotion

6. Determine which messages (aspects) your company and its product/service you want to promote

7. Launch your promotional campaign when all the steps of planning (section D) have been completed

8. Evaluate the results of your promotional efforts

Final thoughts

Promotions are great to generate quick and immediate revenues. Overuse of promotions desensitizes your market. Think about the car dealer that sends out promotions once per month. You know exactly who I'm talking about and I may not even be in your area. Promotions require strategy to be effective.

Client testimony

"My photography business was struggling while I watched others flourish. In my meeting, we discussed running a promotion with prices higher than I normally charged. This was after discussing I was under charging for my services. This promotion took off to the point I had to end the promotion early."

~M.R.

87

To learn the 3 biggest mistakes all business owners make and how to avoid them, visit www.ballistamanagement.com

6

How to Create Repeat Business and Have Clients that Pay, Stay and Refer

When it comes to marketing and generating more income, most business owners are focused outward.

They've carefully established and segmented their target market, and created specific offers and messages for each market segment. They spend thousands of dollars in advertising and direct mail campaigns in hot pursuit of more leads, more customers, and more foot traffic.

While this is an effective way to build a business, it is costly and time consuming. It requires constant and consistent effort, and while this approach does generate results, those results quickly disappear when the effort stops or becomes less intense.

Successful businesses that see sustained growth have a double-edged marketing strategy. They focus their efforts *outward* – on new potential customers and marketing – as well as *inward* – on existing customers and referral business.

These successful businesses have leveraged their existing efforts to generate more revenue. Simply put, their customers buy from them over and over again.

For most businesses, this is the easiest way to increase their revenues. Simple customer loyalty strategies and outstanding customer service are often all you need to dramatically increase your sales – from the customers you already have.

The Cost of Your Customers

Do you know how much it costs your business to buy new customers?

Each new customer that walks through your door – with the exception of referrals – has cost you money to acquire. You have spent money on advertising and promotions to generate leads and turn those leads into customers.

For example, if you have placed an ad in your local newspaper for $1,000, and the ad brings in 10 customers, you have paid $100 to acquire each customer. You would need to ensure each of those customers spent at least $200 to cover your margin and break even.

Alternately, if you spent two hours of your time and $10 per month on an email marketing program to send a newsletter to your existing database of customers, and you bring in 10 customers as a result – each customer has cost you $1.

Generating more repeat business means focusing on the marketing strategies that aim to keep your existing customers instead of purchase new ones – effectively reducing the cost of attracting new customers to your business.

These strategies are simple to implement, and don't require much time investment. Just a solid understanding of how to make customers want to come back and spend more of their money

Keeping Your Customers

Marketing strategies that focus on keeping your current customer base are easy and enjoyable to implement. They allow you to build real relationships with the people you do business with, instead of dealing with a revolving door of people on the other end of your sales process.

Repeat customers create a community of people around your business that presumably share the same needs, desires and frustrations. The information you gain from these customers (market research) can help you strengthen your understanding of your target audience, and more accurately segment it.

Remember – 80% of your revenue comes from 20% of your customers. Always focus on these customers. They are ideal customers that you want to recruit, and hold on to.

To learn the 3 biggest mistakes all business owners make and how to avoid them, visit www.ballistamanagement.com

Customer Service: Make them love buying from you

Every business – even those with excellent service standards can improve the service they provide their customers. Customer service seems to be a dying concept in most businesses; more focus seems to be placed on the speed of the transaction. These days you can even go to the grocery store now and not speak to a single sales associate thanks to self-serve checkouts.

To improve your company's customer service standards, take a survey of your customers and your employees to brainstorm ways you can improve the experience of buying from your business.

Successful customer service standards – those that make your customers *buy* – are:

Consistent. The standards are up kept by every person in your organization. Expectations are clear and followed through. Customers know what to expect, and choose your business because of those expectations.

Convenient. It is nearly effortless for the customer to spend money at your place of business. Convenience can take many forms – location, product selection, value-added services like delivery – and it is also consistent.

Customer-driven. The service the customer receives is exactly how they would like to be treated when buying your product or service. It is reflective of your target market, and appropriate to their lifestyle. Customers would probably not appreciate white linen tablecloths at a fast food restaurant, but they would appreciate a 2-minutes or less guarantee.

To learn the 3 biggest mistakes all business owners make and how to avoid them, visit www.ballistamanagement.com

Newsletters: Keep in touch with your customers

A regular newsletter is an easy, time-effective, and inexpensive marketing strategy to implement. Unfortunately, many small businesses think these are too time consuming and too expensive to adopt as part of their marketing strategy.

The most popular type of newsletter distribution is email. This will cost your business as little at $10 per month for an email marketing service subscription, and can be customized to your unique branding.

Here is an easy five-step process to starting a company newsletter:

1. Pick your audience. New customers? Market segment? Existing customers?

2. Choose what you're going to say. Company news? Feature product? New offer?

3. Determine how you're going to say it. Articles? Bullet points? Pictures?

4. Decide how it's going to get to your audience. Email? Mail? In-store?

5. Track your results. How many people opened it? Read it? Took action?

Value Added Service: Give them happy surprises

Adding value to your business is an effective way of getting your customers back. Every person I know would choose a mattress store that offered free delivery over one that did not. It's that simple.

There are many ways to add value to your business, including:

o **Feature your expertise.** Use your knowledge to provide additional value to your customers. Offer a free consumer guide or report with every purchase.

o **Add convenience services.** Offer a service that makes their purchase easier, or more convenient. The best example of this is free shipping or delivery.

o **Package complementary services**. Packaging like items together creates an increase in perceived value. This is great for start-up kits.

o **Offer new products or services**. Feature top of the line or exclusive products, available only at your business. Offer a new service or profile a new staff member with niche expertise.

Value added services generate repeat customers in one of two ways:

1. Impress them on their first visit. Impress you customer with great service, a product that meets their needs, and then wow them with something extra that they weren't expecting. Get them to associate the experience of dealing with your business with happy surprises, and create a perception of higher value.

93

To learn the 3 biggest mistakes all business owners make and how to avoid them, visit www.ballistamanagement.com

2. Entice them to come back. The introduction of a new value-added service can be enough to convince a customer to buy from you again. Their initial purchase established a trust and knowledge of your business and its processes. They will want to "be included" in anything new you have to offer – especially if there is exclusivity. It is easier to attract clients that have purchased from you than potential clients who have not.

Customer Loyalty Programs: Give them incentives

Another simple way to keep in touch with existing customers and keep them coming back to you is to create a customer loyalty program.

These programs do not have to be complicated or costly, and are relatively easy to maintain once they have been implemented. These programs help you gain more information on your customers and their purchasing habits.

Here are some examples of simple loyalty programs that you can implement:

Free product or service. Give them every 10th (or 6th) product or service free. Produce stamp cards with your logo and contact information on it.

Reward dollars. Give them a certain percentage of their purchase back in money that can only be spent in-store. Produce "funny money" with your logo and brand.

Rewards points. Give them a certain number of points for every dollar they spend. These points can be spent in-store, or on special items you bring in for points only.

To learn the 3 biggest mistakes all business owners make and how to avoid them, visit www.ballistamanagement.com

Membership amenities. Give members access to VIP amenities that are not available to other customers. Produce member cards or give out member numbers.

Remember that in order for this strategy to work, you and your team have to understand and promote it. The program in itself becomes a product that you sell.

Final Thoughts

We cannot stress enough that any one of these will help drive the business you want. Focusing on one at a time allows you to maximize the benefits of that strategy. Once that strategy is up and running, plan the next strategy you want to tackle. One at a time is the key to your success.

Client testimonial

"I had not considered the cost of keeping current customers versus getting new customers. The books I had read kept telling me to focus on attracting new clients. After speaking with Dowuan about our challenges, we came up with a way to reward our current customers. It was exactly opposite of what everyone else was doing. An interesting side effect was that it brought in new clients too, because they wanted to be rewarded for their loyalty. I know run client promotions twice per year!"

~G.S.

To learn the 3 biggest mistakes all business owners make and how to avoid them, visit www.ballistamanagement.com

7

Immediate Sales

If you're a business owner, you're also a salesperson.

You've had to sell the bank to get them to loan you your start-up capital. You've had to sell the best employees on why they should work for your business. You've had to convince your business partner, spouse, and friends why your business idea is a good one.

Now you have to repeatedly sell your product or service to your customers.

The ability to sell effectively and efficiently is one every successful business owner has cultivated, and continues to develop. It can be a complicated and time consuming task; one that you will have to continually work on throughout your career in order to be – and stay – successful.

96

Fortunately, making sales is a step-by-step process that can be learned, customized, and continuously improved. There are a wide range of tools available to help and support your sales efforts.

You don't have to be the most outgoing, enthusiastic person to be successful at sales. You don't even have to be a good public speaker. All you need is an understanding of the basic sales process, and a genuine passion for what you are selling.

Sales 101

As I said before, making sales is a process. There are clear, step-by-step actions that can be taken and result in a sale.

The sales process varies according to the type of business, type of customers and type of product or service that is offered; however, the core steps are the same. Similarly, sales training varies from individual to individual, but the core skills and abilities remain the same.

Here is a basic seven-step process that you can follow, or fine tune to suit your unique products and services. Remember that each step is important, and builds on the step previous. It is essential to become adept at each step, instead of solely focusing on closing the sale.

1. Preparation

Make sure you have prepared for your meeting, presentation, or day on the sales floor. You have complete control of this part of the sales process, so it is important to do everything you can to set the stage for your success.

To learn the 3 biggest mistakes all business owners make and how to avoid them, visit www.ballistamanagement.com

- Understand your product or service inside and out.
- Prepare all the necessary materials, and organize them neatly.
- Keep your place of business tidy and organized. Reface product on shelves.
- Ensure you appear professional and well groomed.
- Do some research on your potential client and brainstorm to find common ground.

2. Build a Relationship

The first few minutes you spend with a potential customer set the stage for the rest of your interaction. First impressions are everything. Your goal in the second step is to relax the customer and begin to develop a relationship with them. Establishing a real relationship with your customer will create trust.

- Make a great first impression: shake hands, make eye contact, and introduce yourself.
- Remain confident and professional, but also personable.
- Mirror their speech and behavior.
- Begin with general questions and small talk.
- Show interest in them and their place of business.
- Notice and comment on positives.
- Find some common ground on which to relate.

98

3. Discuss Needs + Wants

Once you have spent a few moments getting to know your prospect, start asking open-ended questions to discover some of their needs and wants. If they have come to you on the sales floor, ask what brought them in the store. If you are meeting them to present your product or service, ask why they are interested in, or what criteria they have in mind for that product or service.

- If you are making a sales presentation, ask for a few moments at the outset to outline the purpose of your visit, as well as how you have structured the presentation.
- Listen intently, and repeat back information you are not sure you understand.
- Ask open-ended questions to get them talking. The longer they talk, the more insight they are providing you into their needs and purchase motivations.
- Ask clarifying questions about their responses.
- If you become sure the customer is going to buy your product or service, begin to ask questions specific to the offering. i.e., what size/color do you prefer?

4. Present the Solution

Once you have a solid understanding of what they are looking for, or what issue they are looking to resolve, you can begin to present the solution: your product or service.

To learn the 3 biggest mistakes all business owners make and how to avoid them, visit www.ballistamanagement.com

- Explain how your product or service will solve their problem or meeting their needs. If several products apply, begin by presenting the mid-level product.

- Illustrate your points with anecdotes about other happy customers, or awards the product or service has earned.

- Use hypothetical examples featuring your customer. Encourage them to picture a scenario after their purchase.

- Begin by describing the benefits of the product, then follow up with features and advantages.

- Watch your customer's behavior as you speak, and ask further qualifying questions in response to body language and verbal comments.

- Give the customer an opportunity to ask you questions or provide feedback about each product or service after you have described or explained it.

- Ask closed-ended questions to gain agreement.

5. Overcome Objections

As you present the product or service, take note of potential objections by asking open-ended questions and monitoring body language. Expect that objections will arise and prepare for it. Consider brainstorming a list of all potential objections, and writing down your responses.

- Repeat the objection back to the customer to ensure you understand them correctly.
- Empathize with what they have said, and then provide a response that overcomes the objection.
- Confirm that the answer you have provided has overcome their objection by repeating yourself.

The Eight Most Common Objections
The product or service does not seem valuable to me. There is no reason for me to act know. I will wait. It's safest not to make a decision right away. There is not enough money for the purchase. The competitor or another department offers a better product. There are internal issues between people or departments. The relationship with the decision maker is strained. There is an existing contract in place with another business.

6. Close

This is an important part of the sales process that should be handled delicately. Deciding when to close is a judgment call that must be made in the moment during the sale. Ideally, you have presented a solution to their problem, overcome objections, and have the customer in a place where they are ready to buy.

Here are some questions to ask before you close the sale:

- Does my prospect agree that there is value in my product or service?

To learn the 3 biggest mistakes all business owners make and how to avoid them, visit www.ballistamanagement.com

- Does my prospect understand the features and benefits of the product or service?
- Are there any remaining objections that must be handled?
- What other factors could influence my prospect's decision to buy?
- Have I minimized the risk involved in the purchase, and provided some level of urgency?

Once you have determined it is time to make the sale, here are some sample statements you can use to get the process rolling:

- So, should we get started?
- Shall I grab a new one from the back?
- If you just give me your credit card, I can take care of the transaction while you continue browsing.
- When would you like the product delivered?
- We can begin next month if we receive payment by the end of the week.
- Can I email you a draft contract tomorrow?

7. Service + Follow-up

Once you have made the sale, your work is not over. You want to ensure that that customer will become a loyal, repeat customer, and that they will refer their friends to your business.

Ask them to be in your customer database, and keep in touch with regular newsletters. Follow up with a phone call or drop by to ask how they are enjoying the product or service, and if they have any further questions or needs you can assist them with.

This contact opportunity will also allow you ask for a referral, or an up sell. At the very least, it will ensure you are continuing to foster and build a relationship with the client.

Up selling

Up selling is simply inviting your customers to spend more money in your business by purchasing additional products or services. This could include more of the same product, complementary products, or impulse items.

Regardless, up selling is an effective way to increase profits and create loyal clients – without spending any money to acquire the business. These clients are already purchasing from you – which means they perceive value in what you have to offer – so take the information you have gained in the sales process and offer them a little bit more.

You experience up selling on a daily basis. From "do you want fries with that?" to "have you heard about our product protect program?" companies across the globe have tapped into and trained their staff on the value of the up sell.

Up selling is truly rooted in good customer service. If your client purchases a new computer printer, you'll need to make sure they have the cords required to connect it to the computer, regular and photo paper, and color and black and white ink.

To learn the 3 biggest mistakes all business owners make and how to avoid them, visit www.ballistamanagement.com

If you don't suggest these items, they may arrive home and realize they do not have all the materials needed to use the product. They may choose to purchase those materials somewhere closer, cheaper, or more helpful.

Customer education is another form of up selling. What if you customer doesn't realize that you sell a variety of printer paper and stationery in addition to computer hardware like printers? Take every opportunity to educate your customer on the products and services you offer that may be of interest to them.

An effective way of implementing an up sell system into your business is simply by creating add-on checklists for the products or services you offer. Each item has a list of related items that your customer may need. This will encourage your staff to develop the habit of asking for the up sell.

Other up sell strategies can be implemented:

- **At the point of sale**. This is a great place for impulse items like candy, flashlights, nail scissors, etc.
- **In a newsletter**. This is an effective strategy for customer education.
- **In your merchandising**. Place strips of impulse items near related items. For example, paper clips with paper and pens near binders.
- **Over the phone**. If someone is placing an order for delivery, offer additional items in the same shipment for convenience.
- **With new products**. Feature each new product or service that you offer prominently in your business, and ask your staff to mention it to every customer.

To learn the 3 biggest mistakes all business owners make and how to avoid them, visit www.ballistamanagement.com

Sales Team

Employing a team of strong salespeople will benefit your business with the expertise that a seasoned sales person provides.

What Makes a Good Salesperson?

There are a lot of salespeople out there – but what qualities and skills make a great salesperson? These are the attributes you will want to find or develop in your team:

- Willingness to continuously learn and improve sales skills
- Sincerity in relating to customers and providing solutions to their objectives
- An understanding of the company's big picture
- A communication style that is direct, polite, and professional
- Honesty and respect for other team members, customers, as well as the competition.
- Ability to manage time
- Enthusiastic
- Inquisitive
- A great listener
- Ability to quickly interpret, analyze, and respond to information during the sales process
- Ability to connect and develop relationships of trust with potential clients
- Professional appearance

To learn the 3 biggest mistakes all business owners make and how to avoid them, visit www.ballistamanagement.com

Team Building — Keeping Your Team Together

In many businesses, sales is a department or a whole team of people who work together to generate leads and convert customers. Effective management of your sales team is a skill every business owner should cultivate.

Teambuilding, recruitment, and training will be discussed in later sections, but take some time to consider the following aspects of managing a sales team:

Communication

- Are targets and results regularly reviewed?

- Are opportunities for input regularly provided?

- Do sales staff members have a clear understanding of what is expected?

- Do all staff members know daily, weekly, and quarterly targets?

Performance Management

- Are sales staff members motivated to reach targets?

- Are sales staff recognized and rewarded once those targets are reached?

- Are there opportunities for skills training and development?

- Do staff members have broad and comprehensive product or industry knowledge?

To learn the 3 biggest mistakes all business owners make and how to avoid them, visit www.ballistamanagement.com

- Is there opportunity for growth within the company?

- Is performance regularly reviewed?

Operations

- Do you have a solid understanding of your sales numbers (revenue, profit, margins)?

- Are your sales processes regularly reviewed?

- Do you have a variety of sales scripts prepared?

- Do you measure conversion rates?

- How are your leads generated?

Sales Tools

Every salesperson should have an arsenal of tools on hand to assist them in the sales process. These tools can act as aids while a sale is taking place, or help to foster continual learning and development of the salesperson's skills and approach.

Sales tools are not unique to any particular industry. The customization of these tools is what sets a salesperson apart. Experience and know-how add to the effectiveness of each tool.

The list below includes some popular sales tools. Add to this list with other resources that are specific to your business or industry.

To learn the 3 biggest mistakes all business owners make and how to avoid them, visit www.ballistamanagement.com

Tool	Description + Benefit
Scripts	Used for incoming and outgoing telemarketing, cold calls, door-to-door sales, in-store sales Create several different scripts throughout your business Maintains consistency in your sales approach Revise and renew your scripts regularly
Presentation Materials	High-quality information about your product or service Forms: PowerPoint presentation, brochure, product sheets, proposal Serves as an outline of your sales presentation, and keeps you on task
Colleagues	A source of help and advice, especially when you are on the same team or sell similar products Also a source of support
Customer Databases	An accurate, up-to-date database of customer contact information and contact history Used to stay in touch with clients Can also be used for direct mail and follow-up telemarketing
The Internet	A powerful resource for sales help and advice Information to help improve your sales process Online sales coaching Source for product knowledge
Ongoing Training	Constant improvement of your sales skills Constant increase in product knowledge Investment in yourself and your company

8 Tips for Better Sales

To learn the 3 biggest mistakes all business owners make and how to avoid them, visit www.ballistamanagement.com

- **Dress for the sale.** Dress professionally, appear well put together and maintain good hygiene. Ensure you are not only dressed professionally, but *appropriately*. Would your client feel more comfortable if you wore a suit, or jeans and blazer?

- **Speak their language.** Show you understand their industry or culture, and use phrases your customer understands. This may require researching industry jargon or common phrases. Remember to avoid using words and phrases that are used in the sales process: sold, contract, telemarketing, finance, interest, etc. Doing so will help break down the salesperson/customer barrier.

- **Ooze positivity.** Show up or answer the phone with a smile, and leave your personal or business issues behind. Be enthusiastic about what you have to offer, and how that offering will benefit your customer. Reflect this not only in your voice, but also in your body language.

- **Deliver a strong pitch or presentation.** Be confident and convincing. Leave self-doubt at the door, and walk in assuming the sale. Take time to explain complex concepts, and always connect what you're saying to your audience in a specific way.

- **Be a poster-child for good manners.** Accept any amenity you're offered, listen intently, don't interrupt, don't show up late, have a strong handshake, and give everyone you are speaking to equal attention.

To learn the 3 biggest mistakes all business owners make and how to avoid them, visit www.ballistamanagement.com

- **Avoid sensitive subjects**. Politics, religion, swearing, sexual innuendos and racial comments are absolutely off-limits. So are negative comments about other customers or the competition.

- **Create a real relationship.** Icebreakers and small talk are not just to pass the time before your presentation. They are how relationships get established. Show genuine interest in everything your customer has to say. Ask questions about topics you know they are passionate. Speak person to person, not salesperson to customer. Remember everything.

- **Know more than you need to.** Impress clients with comprehensive knowledge – not only of your product or service – but also of the people who use that product or service, and industry trends. Been seen as an expert in order to build trust and respect.

Final thoughts

The sales process is one I fell in love early in life – I was 4 when I made my first sale. This process really has not changed in many years. Understanding the process, customizing it for your personality and product, and executing it repetitively is the key to consistent sales. I will never forget my first client ever (I had not begun consulting officially even). We developed a customized sales process for him which significantly helped his business grow. Ultimately, he was able to sell his business and focus on product creation, which was his passion.

To learn the 3 biggest mistakes all business owners make and how to avoid them, visit www.ballistamanagement.com

8

Profiting from Internet Marketing

Is your business online? If not, it should be.

The internet is today's primary consumer research tool. If your business does not have an online presence, it is harder for customers to find and choose your business over the competition. With over 73% of North Americans online, it is no wonder that individuals and businesses in all industries are looking to the internet to enhance their marketing strategies.

Luckily, it has never been easier to establish and maintain a comprehensive online presence. Internet marketing, also referred to as online marketing, online advertising or e-marketing, is the fastest growing medium for marketing.

But it is not just company websites that users are viewing. Blogs, consumer reviews, chat rooms and a variety of social media are growing rapidly in popularity.

To learn the 3 biggest mistakes all business owners make and how to avoid them, visit www.ballistamanagement.com

The internet is a very powerful tool for businesses if used strategically and effectively. It can be a cost saving alternative to traditional marketing approaches, and may be the most effective way to communicate with your target consumer.

A major advantage of the internet is that you are always open. Users can access your business 24 hours a day, 7 days a week, and depending on your business and the purpose of the website, visitors can also purchase goods at any time.

Internet Marketing for Everyone

The internet is a great way to create product and brand awareness, develop relationships with consumers and share and exchange information. You can't afford not be taking advantage of online marketing opportunities because your competition is likely already there.

Internet marketing can take on many different forms. By creating maintaining a website for your business, you are reaching out to a new consumer base. You can have full control over the messaging that users are receiving and has a global reach.

Internet marketing can be very cost effective. If you have a strong email database of your customers, an e-newsletter may be cheaper and more effective than post mail. You can deliver time sensitive materials immediately and can update your subscribers instantaneously.

To learn the 3 biggest mistakes all business owners make and how to avoid them, visit www.ballistamanagement.com

Top 10 Websites (Globally Jan 2017)

1.	Google	7.	Wikipedia
2.	Facebook	8.	Tencent QQ
3.	YouTube	9.	LinkedIn
4.	Windows Live	10.	Taobao.com
5.	Yahoo	11.	Twitter
6.	Baidu.com		

You will notice that half of these websites are search engines. An increasing number of consumers are first researching products, services and companies online, whether it be to compare products, complete a sale, or look for a future employer. Most people in the 18-35 age group obtain all of their information online—including news, weather, product research, etc. The remaining sites are interactive sites where users can upload information for social networking, or information sharing.

Internet Marketing Strategies

Internet marketing – like all other elements of your marketing campaign – needs to have clear goals and objectives. Creating brand and product awareness will not happen overnight so it is important to budget accordingly, ensuring there is money set aside for maintenance of the website and analytics.

Be flexible with ideas and options—do your research first, try out different options, then test and measure the results. Metrics and evaluations can be updated almost immediately and should be monitored regularly. By keeping an eye out for what online marketing strategies are working and which are not, it will be easier to create a balanced portfolio of marketing techniques.

To learn the 3 biggest mistakes all business owners make and how to avoid them, visit www.ballistamanagement.com

You might find that in certain geographical areas, certain marketing strategies are more effective than others.

This list is by no means the full extent of options available for marketing online, but it is a good place to start when deciding which options are best suited to your company.

Create a website

The primary use for the internet is information seeking, so you should provide consumers with information about your company first hand. You have more control over your branding and messaging and can also collect visitor information to determine what types of internet users are accessing your website.

Search Engine Optimization

Since search engines comprise 50% of the most visited sites globally, you can go through your website to make it more search engine friendly with the aim to increase your organic search listing. An organic search listing refers to listings in search engine results that appear in order or relevance to the entered search terms.

You may wish to repeat key words multiple times throughout your website and write the copy on your site not only with the end reader in mind, but also search engines.

Remember when you design your website that any text that appears in Flash format is not recognized by search engines. If your entire website is built on a Flash platform, then you will have a poor organic search listing.

114

Price Per Click Advertising

If you find that visitors access your website after searching for it first on a search engine, then it may be beneficial to advertise on these websites and bid on keywords associated with your company.

These advertisements will appear at the top of the page or along the left side of the search results on a search engine. You can have control over the specific geographic area you wish to target, set a monthly budget and have the option on only being charged when a user clicks on your link.

Online Directories

Listing your business in an online directory can be an inexpensive and effective online marketing strategy.

However, you need to be able to distinguish your company from the plethora of competitors that may exist. Likely, you will need to complement this strategy with other brand awareness campaigns.

Online Ads (i.e. banner ads on other websites)

These advertisements can have positive or negative effects based on the reputation and consumer perception of the website on which you are advertising. These ads should be treated similar to print ads you may place in local newspapers or other publications. Keeping your company's branding and message clear is also important. No matter where you talk about yourself, you want prospective clients to see the same message.

To learn the 3 biggest mistakes all business owners make and how to avoid them, visit www.ballistamanagement.com

Online Videos

With the growing popularity of sites such as YouTube, it is evident that people love researching online and being able to find video clips of the information they are seeking. Depending on your small business, you may want to upload informational videos or tutorials about your products or services.

Blogging

Blogging can be a fun and interactive way to communicate with users. A blog is traditionally a website maintained by an individual user that has regular entries, similar to a diary. These entries can be commentary, descriptions of events, pictures, videos, and more. Companies can use blogging as a way to keep users updated on current information and allow them to post comments on your blog. If blogging is something you wish to invest in, make sure that it is regularly updated and monitored.

Top 10 Mistakes to Avoid

Failure to measure ROI

Which metrics are you using? Are your visitors actually motivated to purchase or sign up? If the benefits of your online campaign are not greater than the costs incurred, then you may wish to re-evaluate your strategy.

Poor Web Design

This can leave a poor impression of your company on the visitor. A poor design could result in frustration on the visitors' part if they are not able

To learn the 3 biggest mistakes all business owners make and how to avoid them, visit www.ballistamanagement.com

to easily find what they went on your site to search for and also does not build trust. If consumers do not trust your company or your website, you will not be able to complete the sale and develop a longer relationship with that customer. You also need to include privacy protection and security when building trust.

This also includes ensuring all information on the website is current and having customer service available if users are experiencing difficulty or cannot find the information they are seeking. This could be as simple as providing a 'Contact Us' email or phone number for support.

Becoming locked into an advertising strategy early

Remember your marketing mix when creating a marketing strategy and avoid putting all of your eggs in one basket. Online marketing is a very valuable tool, but depending on your business and your target markets, other marketing campaigns may be the best option for you. Especially if this is your first time making a significant investment into your online sector, you want to remain flexible and able to adapt your strategy based off feedback received by researching and analyzing different options.

Acting without researching

Similar to becoming locked into an advertising strategy early, this mistake implies not dutifully testing and researching different online marketing options. For example, if your target consumer is aged 65+ and you are spending all of your marketing efforts into creating a blogging website (where the average ages of bloggers are 18-35), then you are likely not going to have a successful campaign.

To learn the 3 biggest mistakes all business owners make and how to avoid them, visit www.ballistamanagement.com

Assuming more visitors means more sales

You have to go back to your original goals and the purpose of your company. More visitors may not mean more sales if your website is used primarily for information and consumers purchase their products elsewhere. This is also vice versa. You could have an increase in sales without an increase in unique visitors if your current consumer base is very loyal and willing to spend lots of money.

Often people will collect information online about products they wish to purchase because it is easier to compare options, but they purchase in person. Even though shopping online is becoming quite popular, people still prefer to see and feel the physical product before purchasing.

Failing to follow up with customers that purchase

Return sales can account for up to 60% of total revenue. It's no wonder that organizations are always trying to maintain loyal customers and may have customer relationship management systems in place. It is easier to get a happy customer to purchase again than it is to get a new customer to purchase once.

Not incorporating online marketing into the business plan

By ensuring that your online marketing plan is fully integrated and accurately represents your organization's overall goals and objectives, the business plan will be more comprehensive and encompassing. In the United States, 88% of citizens, nearly 290 million individuals, have access to the internet. Not incorporating online marketing hinders the ability to reach this large group of potential prospects.

To learn the 3 biggest mistakes all business owners make and how to avoid them, visit www.ballistamanagement.com

Trying to discover your own best practices

It is very beneficial to use trial and error to determine the best online strategy from your company, but do not be afraid to do your research and learn from what other have already figured out. There will be many cases where someone was in a very similar position as you and they may have some suggestions and secrets that they wish to share. Researching in advance can save a great deal of time and money.

Spending too much too fast

Although it may be cheaper than traditional marketing approaches, internet marketing does have its costs. You have to consider the software and hardware designs, maintenance, distribution, supply chain management, and the time that will be required. You don't want to spend your entire marketing budget all at once.

Getting distracted by metrics that are not relevant

As discussed in the following section, there are endless reports and measurables that you can analyze to determine the effectiveness of your campaign. You will need to establish which measurables are actually relevant to your marketing.

Testing and Measuring Online

As with any element of your marketing campaign, you will need to track your results and measure them against your investment. Otherwise, how will you know if your online marketing is successful?

To learn the 3 biggest mistakes all business owners make and how to avoid them, visit www.ballistamanagement.com

These results - or metrics – need to be recorded and analyzed as to how they impact your overall return on investment.

Some examples of metrics are:

- New account setups
- Conversion rates
- Page stickiness
- Contact us form completion

Due to the popularity in online marketing and the importance of having a strong web presence, companies have demanded more sophisticated tracking tools and metrics for their online activities. It can be very difficult to not only know what to measure, but also HOW to measure.

Thankfully, it is easier than ever to get the information you need with the many types of software and services available, including Google Analytics, which are free and relatively accurate.

8 Metrics to Track

The following are the key measurables to watch for when testing and measuring your internet marketing efforts:

Conversions

How many leads has your online presence generated? Of those leads, how many were turned into sales? How many provided additional information? Ultimately, your campaign needs to have a positive impact on your business.

To learn the 3 biggest mistakes all business owners make and how to avoid them, visit www.ballistamanagement.com

Regardless of the specific purpose of the campaign – from lead generation and service sign-up, to blog entries – you need to know how many customers are taking the desired action in response to your efforts. Your tracking tool will be able to provide you with this information.

Spend

If you are not making a profit – or at least breaking even – from your internet marketing efforts, then you need to change your strategy. Redistribute your financial resources and reconsider your motives and objectives for your online campaign.

An easy way to do this analysis is to divide your total spend by conversions. This could also be broken down by product. You could also use tracking tool and view reports on the 'per visit value of every click,' from every type of source. Your sources can include organic/search engine referrals, direct visit (i.e. person typed your web address into their address bar), or email/newsletter.

Attention

You need to keep a close eye on how much attention you are getting on your website. One of the best ways to analyze this would be to compare unique visitors to page views per visit to time on site. How many people are visiting, how many pages they are viewing, what pages they are viewing, and how much time they are spending on the site.

A unique visitor is any one person who visits the website in a given amount of time. For example, if Evelyn visits her online banking website daily

121

for an entire month, over that one month period, she is considered to be one unique visitor (not 30 visitors).

You may also want to incorporate referring source as well – the places online that refer customers to your website. You'll be able to determine what referring sources offer the 'best' visitors.

Top Referrals

Know who is doing the best job of referring clients to your website – and note how they are doing this. Is it the prominence of the link? Positioning? Reputation of the referring company?

Understanding where the majority of your visitors are coming from will allow you focus on those types of sources when you increase your referral sites. They also allow you to gain a better understanding of your online market – and target audience.

Bounce Rate

The bounce rate is the number of people who visit the homepage of your website, but do not visit other pages. If you have a high bounce rate, you either have all the necessary information on your homepage (this has become more popular as of late), or you are not giving your customers a reason to click further.

In Google Analytics, view the 'content' or 'pages' report and view the column stating bounce rate.

To learn the 3 biggest mistakes all business owners make and how to avoid them, visit www.ballistamanagement.com

Errors

It is very important to track the errors that visitors receive while trying to access or view your website. For example, if someone links to your website, but makes a spelling error in typing the link, your users will see an error page in their browser, and will not ultimately make it to your website.

You can also receive reports on errors that customer's make when trying to type in your website address in their browser. You may wish to buy the domains with common spelling mistakes, and link those addresses to you true homepage. This will increase overall traffic and potential conversions.

Onsite Search Terms

If you have a 'search website' function on your website, it is useful to monitor which terms users are most frequently searching. This can provide valuable insight into the user friendliness of your site and your website's navigation system. This information will be included in the traffic reporting tool.

Bailout Rates

If you provide users with the option to purchase something on your website (i.e. shopping cart), then you can track where along the purchasing process people decided not to go through with the sale.

This could be at the first step of receiving the order summary and total, or further when stating shipping options. By obtaining this information, a company can reorganize or revamp their website to make the sales process more fluid and possibly encourage more purchases.

123

Here are the three main questions you should be asking yourself when evaluating your website presence:

o   Who visits my website?

o   Where do visitors come from?

o   Which pages are viewed?

After asking these questions, what information can be gleaned from the responses? How can you turn those responses into a workable plan to improve your marketing efforts? Where are the gaps in your strategy?

By evaluating your online presence through the scope of the measurable, you will have a good idea of what is working, what is not, and why. Now, you update your plan and implement.

Final thoughts

Internet marketing is a very fluid space. Rules change regularly. Different platforms have different rules and expectations. Keeping up with these changes will allow you to increase the effectiveness of your campaigns. Also, understanding where your ideal clients hang out online is important. Research this. Study up in six months since behavior patterns change. Internet marketing is fantastic, but requires ongoing support.

9

How to Profit from Direct Mail

Every time you mail an existing or potential customer a letter and ask them to respond or take action, you are running a direct-mail campaign.

Direct mail is a marketing strategy that can help you achieve a number of business objectives. From lead generation to customer retention, direct mail campaigns are a highly versatile and relatively cost-effective choice for business promotion.

What you probably don't realize is that direct mail is one of the most targeted marketing strategies you can implement, and one of the easiest to track, measure and analyze results.

It is also one of the most personal. Instead of an advertisement, flyer, newspaper insert or catalogue, you are sending each customer a personalized letter that is tailored to their unique needs and desires.

125

To learn the 3 biggest mistakes all business owners make and how to avoid them, visit www.ballistamanagement.com

Getting the most out of your direct mail campaign is easy. With a laser-sharp mailing list and irresistible offer, your direct mail campaign can easily flood your business with qualified leads.

Let's get started!

A List of Ideal Customers

Unless you spend time carefully crafting a mailing list of ideal customers, you may as well pack and up go home. The success of a direct mail campaign largely rests on the pinpoint accuracy of your mailing list.

The only people you want on your list are your potential "ideal customers." The people who are most likely to buy from you – often and in large volumes – and who are a delight to deal with. They are the type of people who will account for 80% of your revenue, and just 20% of your total customer base.

You have a number of options when you are creating your mailing list:

- **Existing customer database**. This is a list of all of the people who have previously purchased from you. It is important to gather their full contact information at the time of sale so you will be able to get contact them again.

- **Existing leads database**. This is a list of all of the leads that have come through your door, but have not purchased from you. This may include those who responded to your last direct mail campaign, but have not yet become customers.

126

- **Outsourced list**. This is a list that has been purchased from a market research firm, the government, or the post office. These lists are pulled based on demographic information – age, sex, location, income, family structure, etc.

Putting the mailing list together

Once you have determined the source(s) for your mailing list, you will have to spend some time assembling it and preparing it for your mailing.

1. Make sure all contacts are up to date. Phone old contacts to confirm their mailing address. An out-of-date list will cost you money in printing and postage.

2. Ensure all contacts are accurate to the list criteria. Take a read through your list to make sure there are no contacts that shouldn't be on the list.

3. Use a database management program to manage your mailing. This will allow you to keep a master list, and create custom lists for each mailing. Remember to save the file name as something that describes the mailing so you can easily find it.

Writing Effective Direct Mail Pieces

Now that you have a laser-sharp mailing list, you will want to do everything you can to target your message to the recipients on your list. Remember that maintaining your voice and image is important here too.

To learn the 3 biggest mistakes all business owners make and how to avoid them, visit www.ballistamanagement.com

An effective direct mail piece:

- **Has a clear structure.** The piece is clearly a letter – there is an engaging headline, clear message, point form list of benefits, and postscript.

- **Features an irresistible offer.** The purchase opportunity is too good for the target audience to refuse. It includes an element of scarcity and urgency.

- **Focuses on customer benefits.** The customer clearly understands "what's in it for me?" The product or service is clearly positioned as something of value and a solution to a need, problem, or desire.

- **Is personal and conversational.** The letter is personally addressed, and reads as though it was composed specifically for the recipient. It is written in conversational tone, with short sentences and limited description.

- **Is short.** The letter communicates what it needs to, and closes. It does not go on for pages in length. The messages are clear, succinct, and simple.

- **Is urgent.** The piece gets the reader to act immediately. There is a time limit or a quantity limit to the offer that requires an urgent response.

- **Includes a Postscript.** The offer or urgency is repeated after the signature at the bottom of the letter. Like a headline, everyone will read the P.S.

To learn the 3 biggest mistakes all business owners make and how to avoid them, visit www.ballistamanagement.com

The Five-Step Direct Mail Campaign

1. Determine Your Target Audience

As we discussed above, you will want to ensure that you have the most accurate, targeted list possible for your direct mail campaign.

Be clear about the purpose for your direct mail campaign – this will help you decide if you want to send your letters to your entire target market, a segment of that market, existing customers, or potentially a referring business's customers. Then you can determine how you craft your offer, how you structure your letter, and when you choose to send it.

2. Choose what you want to say

What is the message you want to communicate to your target list? What can you offer them that will entice them to act immediately?

Create a specific offer for each direct mail campaign to ensure each time you communicate with your target list you have something new to say. Tailor this offer to each mailing list.

Decide what product or service benefits will be most compelling to your target audience, and include those benefits prominently in your letter.

3. Develop a compelling direct mail piece

You are in control of how your format your message. Are you sending a letter? A brochure and a letter? A postcard? The format of your direct mail piece needs to be tailored to your target list, and reflect your product or service.

To learn the 3 biggest mistakes all business owners make and how to avoid them, visit www.ballistamanagement.com

A younger audience may respond to a postcard, but an older audience may appreciate a formalized letter.

Ensure that whatever format you choose, the piece is professionally designed, prominently includes your logo and company branding, and is professionally produced.

This piece of paper has to act as an ambassador of your company – you absolutely need it to appear impressive and professional.

4. Pick your timing

Some products and purchase decisions are best made at certain times of the year, or the month. If your business or service is seasonal, then there are good times and bad times to try to generate leads. Consider the best purchase windows for the people in your target marketing. When do they get paid? When do they have the money to spend on your product/service? When do they spend the most money?

Anticipate these windows, and time your direct mail campaign accordingly. If you run a lawn sprinkler installation system and summer is your peak season, run a direct mail campaign mid-way through spring, and at the beginning of summer.

Some common time windows include:

- Holiday season (November – December)
- Fridays (paydays)
- The 15th and 30th of every months (also paydays)

To learn the 3 biggest mistakes all business owners make and how to avoid them, visit www.ballistamanagement.com

- Seasons (Spring, Summer, Fall, Winter)
- Financial cycles (year-end, tax time)
- Sports seasons (hockey, football, baseball, etc.)

5. Follow up

Comprehensive follow up to a direct mail campaign means two things:

1. Following up on your letter with a phone call or second letter

Often it takes more than a letter to get a potential customer to take action. This can be a result of the accuracy of your mailing list, your offer, the time of the year, or the quality of the marketing material (brochure). If you are certain that your mailing list is accurate and up to date, follow up to the piece with a phone call, or send another letter.

2. Recording, measuring and analyzing your results.

It is essential that you evaluate each direct mail campaign based on your time investment, financial investment, and your rate of response. How else will you be able to tell if it was a successful or effective strategy?

For each campaign, record and analyze the following information:

- Number of letters sent
- Number or responses as a percentage
- Number of sales directly resulting from the campaign
- Number of enquiries
- Total value of sales directly resulting from the campaign

Based on this information, determine if the campaign was successful (did it make you money?) or not. What made the campaign successful (or not)? Did it target your ideal clients? Was the message direct enough? Did the offer speak to the prospects? Was the branding off? Consider making some changes to your list, your offer, or the piece itself, and try again.

Final thoughts

Direct mail is one of the oldest forms of marketing. Typical response rates vary by industry but are generally pretty low. The reason response is low is because they are not following these rules. These rules are intended to do one thing only – engage the prospects from the moment they see the ad. This engagement is what drives results.

Client testimony

"As a specialty contractor, getting word out to the right prospects is critical. My customized work is not for everyone. By designing a custom direct mail campaign with my ideal client in mind, we were able to increase our sales during our slow season significantly. I believe the work we did on targeting the right areas and the professional help on designing the ad itself really made the difference."

~L.G.

To learn the 3 biggest mistakes all business owners make and how to avoid them, visit www.ballistamanagement.com

10

Creating a Powerful Offer

I'm not going to beat around the bush on this one:

Your offer is the granite foundation of your marketing campaign.

Get it right, and everything else will fall into place. Your headline will grab readers, your copy will sing, your ad layout will hardly matter, and you will have customers running to your door.

Get it wrong, and even the best looking, best-written campaign will sink like the Titanic.

A powerful offer is an irresistible offer. It's an offer that gets your audience frothing at the mouth and clamoring over each other all the way to your door. An offer that makes your readers pick up the phone and open their wallets.

Irresistible offers make your potential customers think, "I'd be crazy not to take him up on that," or "An offer like this doesn't come around very

133

often." They instill a sense of emotion, of desire, and ultimately, urgency.

Make it easy for customers to purchase from you the first time, and spend your time keeping them coming back.

I'll say it again: **Get it right, and everything else will fall into place.**

The Crux of Your Marketing Campaign

As you work your way through this program, you will find that nearly every chapter discusses the importance of a powerful offer as related to your marketing strategy or promotional campaign.

There's a reason for this. The powerful offer is more often than not the reason a customer will open their wallets. It is how you generate leads, and then convert them into loyal customers. The more dramatic, unbelievable, and valuable the offer is the more dramatic and unbelievable the response will be.

Many companies spend thousands of dollars on impressive marketing campaigns in glossy magazines and big city newspapers. They send massive direct mail campaigns on a regular basis; yet don't receive an impressive or massive response rate.

These companies do not yet understand that simply providing information on their company and the benefits of their product is not enough to get customers to act. There is no reason to pick up the phone or visit the store, *right now*.

Your powerful, irresistible offer can:

- Increase leads
- Drive traffic to your website or business
- Move old product
- Convert leads into customers
- Build your customer database

What Makes a Powerful Offer?

A powerful offer is one that makes the most people respond, and take action. It gets people running to spend money on your product or service.

Powerful offers nearly always have an element of *urgency* and of *scarcity*. They give your audience a reason to act immediately, instead of put it off until a later date.

Urgency relates to time. The offer is only available until a certain date, during a certain period of the day, or if you act within a few hours of seeing the ad. The customer needs to act now to take advantage of the offer.

Scarcity is related to quantity. There are only a certain number of customers who will be able to take advantage of the offer. There may be a limited number of spaces, a limited number of products, or simply a limited number of people the business will provide the offer to. Again, this requires that customer act immediately to reap the high value for low cost.

To learn the 3 biggest mistakes all business owners make and how to avoid them, visit www.ballistamanagement.com

Powerful offers also:

Offer great value. Customers perceive the offer as having great value – more than a single product on its own, or the product at its regular price. It is clear that the offer takes the reader's needs and wants into consideration.

Make sense to the reader. They are simple and easy to understand if read quickly. Avoid percentages – use half off or 2 for 1 instead of 50% off. There are no "catches" or requirements; no fine print.

Seem logical. The offer doesn't come out of thin air. There is a logical reason behind it – a holiday, end of season, anniversary celebration, or new product. People can get suspicious of offers that seem "too good to be true" and have no apparent purpose.

Provide a premium. The offer provides something extra to the customer, like a free gift, or free product or service. They feel they are getting something extra for no extra cost. Premiums are perceived to have more value than discounts.

Remember that when your target market reads your offer, they will be asking the following questions:

1. What are you offering me?

2. What's in it for me?

3. What makes me sure I can believe you?

4. How much do I have to pay for it?

To learn the 3 biggest mistakes all business owners make and how to avoid them, visit www.ballistamanagement.com

The Most Powerful Types of Offers

Decide what kind of offer will most effectively achieve your objectives. Are you trying to generate leads, convert customers, build a database, move old product off the shelves, or increase sales?

Consider what type of offer will be of most value to your ideal customers – what offer will make them act quickly.

Free Offer

This type of offer asks customers to act immediately in exchange for something free. This is a good strategy to use to build a customer database or mailing list. Offer a free consultation, free consumer report, or other item of low cost to you but of high perceived value.

You can also advertise the value of the item you are offering for free. For example, act now and you'll receive a free consultation, worth $75 dollars. This will dramatically increase your lead generation, and allow you to focus on conversion when the customer comes through the door or picks up the phone.

The Value Added Offer

Add additional services or products that cost you very little, and combine them with other items to increase their attractiveness. This increases the perception of value in the customer's mind, which will justify increasing the price of a product or service without incurring extra hard costs to your business.

137

Package Offer

Package your products or services together in a logical way to increase the perceived value as a whole. Discount the value of the package by a small margin, and position it as a "start-up kit" or "special package." By packaging goods of mixed values, you will be able to close more high-value sales. For example: including a free desk-jet printer with every computer purchase.

Premium Offer

Offer a bonus product or service with the purchase of another. This strategy will serve your bottom line much better than discounting. This includes 2 for 1 offers, offers that include free gifts, and in-store credit with purchases over a specific dollar amount.

Urgency Offer

As I mentioned above, offers that include an element of urgency enjoy a better response rate, as there is a reason for your customers to act immediately. Give the offer a deadline or limit the number of spots available.

Guarantee Offer

Offer to take the risk of making a purchase away from your customers. Guarantee the performance or results of your product or service, and offer to compensate the customer with their money back if they are not satisfied. This will help overcome any fear or reservations about your product, and make it more likely for your leads to become customers.

To learn the 3 biggest mistakes all business owners make and how to avoid them, visit www.ballistamanagement.com

Create Your Powerful Offer

1. Pick a single product or service.

Focus on only one product or service – or one product or service *type* – at a time. This will keep your offer clear, simple, and easy to understand. This can be an area of your business you wish to grow, or old product that you need to move off the shelves.

2. Decide what you want your customers to do.

What are you looking to achieve from your offer? If it is to generate more leads, then you'll need your customer to contact you. If it is to quickly sell old product, you'll need your customer to come into the store and buy it. Do you want them to visit your website? Sign up for your newsletter? How long do they have to act? Be clear about your call to action, and state it clearly in your offer.

3. Dream up the biggest, best offer.

First, think of the biggest, best things you could offer your customers – regardless of cost and ability. Don't limit yourself to a single type of offer, combine several types of offers to increase value. Offer a premium, plus a guarantee, with a package offer. Then take a look at what you've created, and make the necessary changes so it is realistic.

4. Run the numbers.

Finally, make sure the offer will leave you with some profit – or at least allow you to break even. You don't want to publish an outrageous offer

To learn the 3 biggest mistakes all business owners make and how to avoid them, visit www.ballistamanagement.com

that will generate a tremendous number of leads, but leave you broke. Remember that each customer has an acquisition cost, as well as a lifetime value. The amount of their first purchase may allow you to break even, but the amount of their subsequent purchases may make you a lovely profit.

Wrapping it up

This is the culmination of our book. Leverage the knowledge gained in the previous nine chapters to purposefully and carefully craft your powerful message. From your sales script to online ads, talking to your referral sources and your current prospects, all areas of your marketing can come together to create your message. Use all of the tools at your disposal and watch your leads and sales grow!

So What Do You Do From Here?

Take Action! If you're already an accomplished business owner and earning in excess of $250,000.00 per year (rich according to the Federal Government), use this book as direction to enhance the speed of your business success. If you are not as accomplished as you would like to be then the smartest thing to do is...

A) Call us

B) E-mail us

C) Visit www.ballistamanagement.com

Concentrate on strategies to **LEARN** and the **EARN** will follow! If you are serious about taking the next step, then go to work on yourself, study other business successes, understand marketing strategies, and become a sponge for new (proven) material. The amazing thing about the game of business is that when you put proven processes to work, and continue to follow them, an abundance of success will follow. The biggest mistake is to start a process and then fallback into your old habits after a short time.

Above all, get the knowledge you need before you step onto the field. Think about it, if you were going to challenge Michael Jordan to a game of H.O.R.S.E. for money, wouldn't it make sense to learn the game and practice before you stepped on the court to play him? It is amazing to me how many new small business people start the game of business against seasoned professionals (the competition), without first developing the necessary

141

To learn the 3 biggest mistakes all business owners make and how to avoid them, visit www.ballistamanagement.com

knowledge to be successful. Then they fail and blame the market, the economy, their location, etc.

If you have a business and have not started to create the wealth and systems that allow you to take time off, build retirement accounts, or pay for your children's college, then learn and master the steps outlined in my book. I am a huge advocate of education and mentorships. Get the right information, find someone that knows how to walk you through them, and watch your quality of life take new shape.

Yours in Success,

~Dowuan Proctor and Adolfo Morales

To learn the 3 biggest mistakes all business owners make and how to avoid them, visit www.ballistamanagement.com